10637343

# Lord, How Did I Get This Old So Soon?

## Karen O'Connor

**Guideposts**

New York

Unless otherwise indicated, Scripture quotations are from the Holy Bible, New International Version®, NIV®. Copyright © 1973, 1978, 1984, 2011 by Biblica, Inc.® Used by permission. All rights reserved worldwide.

Verses marked NLT are taken from the Holy Bible, New Living Translation, copyright © 1996, 2004, 2007 by Tyndale House Foundation. Used by permission of Tyndale House Publishers, Inc., Carol Stream, Illinois 60188. All rights reserved.

Verses marked NASB are taken from the New American Standard Bible®, © 1960, 1962, 1963, 1968, 1971, 1972, 1973, 1975, 1977, 1995 by The Lockman Foundation. Used by permission. (www.Lockman.org)

Verses marked NCV are taken from the New Century Version®. Copyright © 2005 by Thomas Nelson, Inc. Used by permission. All rights reserved.

Verses marked AMP are taken from The Amplified Bible, Copyright © 1954, 1958, 1962, 1964, 1965, 1987 by The Lockman Foundation. All rights reserved. Used by permission. (www.Lockman.org)

Guideposts a Church Corporation has made every effort to trace the ownership of all poems and quotes. In the event of a question arising from the use of a poem or quote, we regret any error made and will be pleased to make the necessary correction in future editions of this book.

Cover illustration © Dugan Design Group/Cedric Hohnstadt
Cover design by Dugan Design Group, Bloomington, Minnesota
Additional design by W Design Group, LLC
Typeset by Aptara, Inc.

**LORD, HOW DID I GET THIS OLD SO SOON?**
Copyright © 2014 by Karen O'Connor
Published by Guideposts a Church Corporation
39 Old Ridgebury Road, Suite 27
Danbury, CT 06810
Guideposts.org

This Guideposts edition is published by special arrangement with Harvest House Publishers.

**All rights reserved.** No part of this work may be reproduced or transmitted in any form or by any means, except as may be expressly permitted by the U.S. Copyright Law. For Permissions contact: PermissionsEditor@guideposts.org

**Printed in the United States of America**

10 9 8 7 6 5 4 3 2 1

*For Marjorie,
my inspiration and, through example,
my writing mentor.*

# Contents

A Note from Karen

 Spring / 11

Summer / 53

Autumn / 91

Winter / 139

*The righteous will flourish like a palm tree,*
*they will grow like a cedar of Lebanon;*
*planted in the house of the LORD,*
*they will flourish in the courts of our God.*
*They will still bear fruit in old age,*
*they will stay fresh and green,*
*proclaiming, "The LORD is upright;*
*he is my Rock, and*
*there is no wickedness in him."*

PSALM 92:12-15

# A Note from Karen

Dear Reader:

Do you ever look in the mirror and shout, "Lord, how did I get this old so soon?"

I have. Many times—especially on my birthday.

This question is kind of silly, though, since I'm in my eighth decade. My life didn't happen in a flash. It took time—lots of time. Just as yours did. Maybe like me, you remember clearly what it felt like to be eighteen getting ready for your first prom, going off to college or trade school, walking down the aisle to wed your sweetheart, and then holding your child for the first time. Moments and events that took years now come together in our minds as though they occurred just yesterday, and we wonder where the time went.

Today, with fewer years ahead of me than behind, I decided to write this book of reflections and prayers to share with those of you who might be looking in the mirror and asking God the same question I have.

I find it especially comforting to talk to God at this stage of life. There are no rules, no special words, and no taboos. God is always there, no matter what. We can talk about the ups and downs—the challenges as well as the moments of gratitude that fill each day—regardless of where we are in life. Nothing is off limits to our God of love, forgiveness, and understanding.

Because my prayer life often changes with the seasons, I divided the book into these four sections: Spring—giving rise to hope and new aspirations; Summer—days of warmth and rest; Autumn—a time to quiet ourselves and reflect; and Winter—a season to hunker down and huddle while nature hibernates.

In these pages, you'll find musings and prayers about everyday happenings with family and friends, long-held secrets, and the simple blessings of everyday life that seem more precious and meaningful as we grow older. Taking a walk hand-in-hand with our mates, a grandchild on our lap—content with a hug and a book, and time spent with a close friend after a frightening medical diagnosis.

I hope you will feel encouraged, through whatever season you're experiencing, to share with God your innermost thoughts and feelings—even those you might be ashamed of or scared to admit—and to let God guide you to the peace and contentment you're looking for. As noted author Marjorie Holmes said so many years ago in her best-selling book of the same title, "I've got to talk to somebody, God."

I can't think of anyone I'd rather talk with than our Lord, who is there for us regardless of our age or what we're going through. After a good chat, we may find the question "Lord, how did I get this old so soon?" giving way to a statement. "Thank you, Lord, for the gift of life all these years."

*Karen O'Connor*
*Watsonville, California*

# Spring

*Ask the LORD for rain in the spring,*
*for he makes the storm clouds.*
*And he will send showers of rain*
*so every field becomes a lush pasture.*

ZECHARIAH 10:1 NLT

*"I enjoy the spring more than the autumn now.*
*One does, I think, as one gets older."*

Virginia Woolf

## Spring Fever

Lord, it's springtime, and I'm in love with you and your creation. I spent the morning in the yard pulling weeds with all my might, clipping dangling limbs from heavy-laden shrubs, picking flowers for a vase in the kitchen, and settling back with a glass of ice water to gaze at the azalea bush nudging pink blooms out of their cozy cocoons. As I watch the bees buzz and flit from one plant to another, I feel lazy by comparison. My, they are busy!

## Wash Day

The washing machine is whirling socks, shirts, and sheets into submission as my husband stands guard. He's the official laundry person in our house. I'm laughing, Lord, at the memory of the day he proposed—stating one condition—that *he* be in charge of wash day during our marriage. I hesitated for a split second and then said yes to his proposal and his condition.

Here we are 30 years later, and it's still "Charles in charge." His mother taught him well, and I thank her for it. Every few days I see a fresh stack of clean and folded clothing ready to put into drawers and on hangers. I never worry that I'll run out of clean items to wear.

This reminds me of your goodness, dear God. You supply all my needs in Christ Jesus because you know what I need even before I do. Thank you for my husband and for your Son, Jesus.

## Drawing a Line

Lord, my friend called today and told me she and her husband are going broke supporting their wayward son and his wife. The young couple can't seem to hold jobs and don't seem to care. They've moved in without an end time in sight. I know it's important to help family members when they're in trouble, but when do we draw the line? My friends are in their seventies and need what savings they have to make it through the rest of their lives. Now they're draining their resources by assuming responsibility for others.

Can you sense my frustration? Maybe it's because I've been a "helper" too. I remember buying my son a desk, a car, a uniform, and dress clothes for a new sales job. I'm glad I could lend a hand, but the truth is I overdid it. I later learned that what he most needed from me was love and prayer support. Yes, material things are important too because a person can't land a job on a mother's love alone, but I was too quick to resolve his dilemmas instead of supporting him as he worked through the problems on his own.

Today my son is a successful and self-confident businessman in his own right. He's paying his bills, taking care of his family, and even hiring me to do some writing for him. And I'm taking care of my finances so I won't have to lean on him unnecessarily.

Thank you, Lord, for teaching me the difference between "taking over" and "taking care" through prayer.

## Unto Dust

Today, Lord, I'm thinking about spring cleaning. Not that this is the only time I clean, but there seems to be something special about springtime. It represents new beginnings, starting over, shaping things up, airing out rooms, and polishing furniture. It's more than just passing over the rooms with a feather duster.

You know I don't like to dust. It's not that difficult, but it seems so fruitless. If I dust on Monday, the little particles sneak back on Tuesday. If I ignore them on Tuesday, the pile is higher on Wednesday. And yet we can't live in a cloud of dust. I put off this uninspiring work one more day and then give in and just do it.

Maybe I should don a new attitude, remembering that you created humankind from dust and unto dust we shall return when our time on earth is over. I should look at dust with respect for what it represents. I will let it remind me of you instead of despising its endless return. I'll do that, dear God, and maybe it will lighten this inevitable task.

## Personal Space

"Am I bothering you with all my little noises and chores?" my husband asked as I worked in our home office.

"No, not at all—as long as you don't talk to me," I responded. "I need to concentrate."

Five minutes later...

"Hon, should I save these papers from the bank regarding our mortgage?" Charles asked as he handed them to me.

"No. You can shred them," I replied, handing them back.

Two minutes later...

"My brother sent me the funniest email forward. Do you have a couple of spare minutes to look at it?"

"Not really. I'm trying to make this a workday. Send it over, and I'll take a look tomorrow."

"Looks like I sent it to the kids but forgot to add your name. I'll try again. Okay, here it comes."

"Thanks."

"Guess what? Now that we've refinanced the house and added an extra payment at the end of each year, we're killing this thing. Great, huh!" he said with a big smile.

*Lord, what do I need to say to make it clear that I need quiet?* I prayed silently. And I'm not the only one. I read an article in the paper this week that said one of the greatest challenges couples face is lack of personal space. I get that. I remember my mother going bananas with my dad in their later years. He loved to tell people that he never wanted her to be farther away from him than an arm's length. She, on the other hand, had a football field in mind. After 50-some years of marriage, 25 years of raising four children, and the same number of years having her father live with our family, Mom wanted—make that *needed*—time alone to think and pray and *be*. I do too!

## Yard Sales

Springtime may be a season of blooms and blossoms, but it's also a time to de-clutter the closets and sell off the stuff I probably shouldn't have purchased in the first place. On Saturday mornings cars move into our neighborhood like a parade of ants across a picnic table as families eye front yards packed with clothes, toys, kitchen gadgets, old CDs, videos, and books—all for sale at bargain prices. Which one appears enticing enough to make them stop, shop, and part with their cash?

I'm an interested observer. I can't be bothered participating even though I might be missing out on some great deals. What I enjoy is seeing people haggle with one another—begging for a discount of a nickel or a dime on a 50-cent item.

But maybe I do haggle with you, God, so you'll let me off the hook from my 50-cent sins—a catty word here, a misstep there, a bitter thought this morning, a withheld compliment this afternoon.

"Are they really so bad?" I ask. "It's not like I'm a murderer or a tax evader." You listen and then remind me gently that *any* sin against another person is a sin against you. You call me to *your* standards, not mine. The bar I set for myself is always lower than the one you set for me. Thank you for using neighborhood yard sales to teach me this lesson once again.

## Having Doubts

Lord, I remember a time in my life when I didn't know what to believe. I was slogging my way through a forest of beliefs and religious philosophies. One week I attended a Catholic Mass. Another week I visited a Religious Science service. And on yet another Sunday I sat in the back row at a Presbyterian Church. I was determined to learn about you, God, and to ask you to remove my doubt.

I was certain of two things. I needed hope and help. Then on a Monday morning, while returning from a run along the beach, I plopped down on a bench and shouted to you over the waves, begging you to reveal yourself to me. As soon as I finished my plea, the words in John 14:6 came to me with fresh meaning: *"I am the way and the truth and the life. No one comes to the Father except through me."* At that moment my doubt vanished and was replaced with the living words of you, Jesus Christ. I knew then that *you are the way* to God the Father, and you would guide me to the answers I was looking for. I longed for peace, and I was very sure I wouldn't be able to achieve it on my own. I didn't know what lay ahead, but I was excited to find out by focusing on what you promised in your Word, the Bible. I made a commitment then to join a Bible-teaching church, to study Scripture, and to ask questions. And you have been faithful to answer me all the days since.

Your Word also says, *"Ask and it will be given to you; seek and you will find; knock and the door will be opened to you*" (Matthew 7:7). Dear God, I pray that anyone who is in doubt will stop right now and turn to you in prayer. I know they will be satisfied and find answers because you will not desert them. You will hear them and answer. Amen.

## Forget-Me-Not

This lovely little flower has flat, five-lobed petals in blue, pink, or white with yellow centers. A German legend claims that you, Lord, were naming all the plants when a tiny, yet-unnamed-one cried out, "Forget me not, O Lord!" And you replied, "That shall be your name!"

I feel like that small, spring blossom sometimes—especially as I grow older. Looking around me at the grocery store, the fitness center, in church pews, and at the movie theater, it seems *everyone* is younger than I am. Of course, that's not entirely true. There are a few gray heads (some blue ones too!) here and there, but the majority of people are between the ages of 20 and 50—and they run the world now. Even my kids are slipping into the downside of middle age. Two are in their fifties, and one more will hit that mark next year! How can this be? Didn't I just carry them home from the hospital, see them off to kindergarten with tears in my eyes, watch them graduate from high school and college just last month, and then give them away in marriage to their sweethearts last week?

O God, forget me not as I grow older. Life is ebbing away too fast for me to keep up.

# Breakfast with Bees

This morning, Lord, my husband and I carried our oatmeal and fruit outside to eat at the table with a view of our prayer garden. The bees arrived before us! They were feasting on the violet blooms covering the ground on either side of the flagstone walkway that leads to the birdbath. I enjoyed seeing and hearing them at work. They do buzz!

I looked around at the lovely flowers and shrubs my husband has planted and tended over the years. If it weren't for him, we wouldn't have what we have in our yard. As the plaque in the corner reads, "Though an old man, I am a young gardener." How true! Charles comes to life when he puts his gloved hands in the dirt to turn the soil and place annuals and perennials here and there. The words on another plaque capture my attention: "The best place to find God is in a garden." Oh yes, Lord, it is the best place. When I am among your creation I am closest to you and happiest within myself. Thank you for your bounty.

# A New Hope

I read this verse today: *"In his great mercy [God] has given us new birth into a living hope through the resurrection of Jesus Christ from the dead, and into an inheritance that can never perish, spoil or fade"* (1 Peter 1:3-4). O Lord, what a promise! What joy it gives me to read those words and make them mine. No matter what comes my way as I grow older and, in time, am less able to do the things I can do now, I will carry that hope with me. Through your resurrection I am made new and ageless. I have an eternal inheritance that will never diminish. I feel younger already! I have a new spring in my step and a new song in my heart. Thank you for loving me so much.

## Dinner for Six at Seven

Lord, as I think about what to serve our guests tonight, I'm reminded of a funny story I heard about an elderly man and woman. They agreed to meet for dinner at the corner of Seventh Avenue and Central at six o'clock. They never did get together because the man showed up at the corner of Sixth and Central at seven o'clock and the woman, waiting in the correct spot, decided he'd stood her up.

Oh, these older years! They're filled with mishaps like that. Hearing aids, helpful as they can be, don't always do the job.

Now back to my dinner party. I want to make something tasty but easy to prepare. Soup and a green salad maybe? Pasta and veggies? Sandwiches and chips? Then I remember that one man can't handle pasta, another is sensitive to soup because of the salt, sandwiches are difficult for one woman with dentures, and another doesn't like veggies. Okay, blitz the menu. We'll take the crowd to a local coffeehouse, pay for everyone to order what they want, and come back to our house for an after-dinner coffee on the patio. Case closed!

## Bills, Bills

Lord, bills are as predictable as spring rain. Utilities, phone, television, and Internet bills keep coming. And of course there are groceries, dry cleaning, clothing, shoe repairs, fuel for our vehicles, insurance, homeowner association dues, and much more to pay for week after week, month after month.

Sometimes I resist looking at our bank statements. I fear we won't have enough money to cover everything. I can't work as hard as I used to. My husband is retired—and deservedly so after working until age 78. I throw up my hands in worry or bury my head in fear—but it doesn't help. It only drives me to desperation. *Enough!*

I turn to you, Lord, and read in your Word and find assurance and comfort. Thank you!

*He provides food for those who fear him; he remembers his covenant forever* (Psalm 111:5).

*The LORD will open the heavens, the storehouse of his bounty, to send rain on your land in season and to bless all the work of your hands* (Deuteronomy 28:12).

*Seek first [God's] kingdom and his righteousness, and all these things will be given to you as well* (Matthew 6:33).

*My God will meet all your needs according to the riches of his glory in Christ Jesus* (Philippians 4:19).

# The Good Old Days?

My computer wouldn't shut down last night. Lord, I panicked! I tried everything I'd read about on the Internet. No success. I'm in the middle of writing a book, and I can't be interrupted with technical issues or—worse yet—having to buy a new computer. Oh for the "good old days" when I used a typewriter for my manuscripts. All I had to do was change the ribbon when the ink ran out and get the machine lubricated once a year or so. Then came electric typewriters, followed by word processors, and finally the personal computer arrived. Now it's a laptop or tablet or smart phone! All of these creations are ready to serve their owners, but when they become cranky or decide to retire, users are in hot water right away.

On the other hand, computers have many advantages. I like the ease of typing, the friendly interface, and the fact that I can write my books and articles from anywhere at any time—a coffee shop, a hotel, a park, in my yard sitting cross-legged on the grass or under an umbrella at the picnic table. Maybe the good old days weren't so good after all. Thank you for advances in technology.

*An update, Lord:* I resolved the computer dilemma. I remembered (Did you prompt me?) that I could hold down the [START] button for 10 seconds and the computer would shut off. When I booted up the next day, I saw what went wrong—a "background" program hadn't closed properly. Whew!

## Balancing Act

I remember reading a news story about the famous high-wire artist Nik Wallenda fulfilling his lifelong dream of walking a wire 200 feet above the raging waters of Horseshoe Falls, the largest of the three falls that make up Niagara Falls. It took him 30 minutes. When a reporter asked how he felt out there, Nik was quick to say he was very peaceful during the walk. "I prayed nonstop," he added.

Lord, this reminds me of how I feel sometimes. Life is a balancing act, and I'm carrying a lot heavier burden than Wallenda's 40-pound balance pole. There are chores to look after, children and grandchildren to relate to, a husband to communicate with, and a house and yard to maintain. And what about me? I have to take care of myself too, paying attention to diet, and exercise, and prayer, and friendships.

With you ahead of me, behind me, beside me, and within me, I too am at peace. I know I will arrive at the other side at the right time without missing a step. Thank you, Lord, for leading the way. In the springtime of my life you inspire me to get a move on, followed by summer where I come into full bloom, then autumn sets in and I slow down, until finally, in the winter of my life, I can fully rest in you and trust you to provide whatever I need.

## Across the Desk

Lord, I wasn't sure this was going to work out—having my husband's desk and my desk facing each other in our small office. But it's been six years, and we're still talking! In fact, it's working out so much better than when we were in different rooms. As my husband's hearing diminishes, it's a lot easier to sit across from one another. If he can't hear me, he can read my lips.

When I'm working on a book, he's usually respectful and maintains the silence I need. It's also a good way to work on finances, discuss our calendars, and make plans for the day, week, and month.

Mostly, I enjoy having him nearby because I'm so aware that someday one of us will be missing. A desk will be empty, and the room will be a quiet reminder of what we once shared. Please help me count each day precious and enjoy the time Charles and I have together. When little annoyances creep up, help me sweep them aside and focus on the blessings we have.

## Flowers and Tears

Our neighbor Bob stopped by today, Lord, holding out a bunch of handpicked flowers from his garden. "Will you watch my house and take care of my flowers while I go out of town to visit my grandson?" he asked in a playful tone.

"Of course!" I assured him it would be my pleasure. He'd done similar favors for us when we traveled.

He handed me a scrap of paper with his phone number written on it in case of an emergency.

I like living in this close-knit neighborhood with other "mature" men and women. As one man said the day we took residence in our new house, "Let's take care of each other."

Within two years his wife died of cancer, and we all rallied around him, never imagining that one of us would leave our community so soon. Flowers and cards poured in and tears flowed while the man absorbed our love and care.

My husband said quietly, "More of us will go before too many more years pass. It could be one of us." He squeezed my hand.

His words rocked my world. I didn't want to think about that. I was still enjoying the newness of our lovely retirement home with the front porch and flower-decked backyard, the interior with hardwood floors and high ceilings and windows that let in the warm sunlight.

And yet there it was—the truth. We may be blessed with additional years together with neighbors and friends or you may call us to our heavenly home unexpectedly. But while I'm here, I'm going to do what I can to care for my neighbors, your gifts to me.

## A Lick and a Promise

It's that day of the week again—time to tidy up the bathrooms. For years I didn't mind, but now it feels like drudgery. Why does my husband have to splash the mirror and glass along with his face? I just spritzed the surface and wiped it clean. Can't he see that? No, because he just messed it up!

I wish I could laugh at all this. What does it matter anyway in the big scheme of life. It's just a bathroom—a toilet, a sink, and a mirror. And yet it does. I like things to stay clean and orderly. I seem to be made to prefer that. But then again, you made me and my husband and every other human being. We're all as unique as the snowflakes that fall from the sky. So how can I assume that my way is the best way? It's just *one* way.

Now that I think more about this, I'm going to make a new choice—to give my bathroom a "good enough" cleaning. It doesn't have to be perfect. I could let things slide a bit, relax, take a step back and a look around. Life won't stop just because of a few splashes on the mirror. But life will get messy if I make a *big* deal out of things that are small in importance. Help me, dear Lord, to keep a healthy perspective.

## Discovering Ireland

Lord, as you know, ever since I was a "wee lass," I've wanted to put my feet on the soil where my ancestors were born and raised. Thank you that this year I was able to do so. And what a time it was to walk the streets of Dublin, the birthplace of my grandparents, and to ride the country roads from one village to the next. Charles and I loved taking in the sights and sounds of this beautiful country. I can't imagine heaven being any more magnificent, yet I know it will be because you've said that no words can describe what you have planned for us on the other side of life on earth. How gracious you are to prepare a place for your people. I feel humbled and excited just thinking about it.

## Body Beautiful

Lord, you tell us in the Bible that we are fearfully and wonderfully made. I'm happy to read those words because at times I've been critical of my body, wishing I had more hair on my head and less cellulite on my thighs. Today I'm giving up the wishes and wants and if onlys! I choose to embrace what you've given me. This spring instead of trying to shape up for summer, as the ads from magazines and newspapers shout, I will be content with where I am, with what I have, and with who I am. I will be grateful that I can see, and hear, and walk, and think, and feel, and sing, and type, and cook, and play. May I never abuse or take for granted this wonderful gift of a healthy and fit physical body that has served me for more than 70 years. Thank you, dear God. May I use it to glorify you.

## Sartu

Today I'm looking at a photo of young Sartu from Ethiopia. Thank you, Lord, for bringing her into our lives through the ministry of Compassion. I love knowing that our few dollars a month enable her to go to school, to have clothing and shoes and books, and, most important, to learn about your love for her. It's humbling to see how much can be accomplished with so little. But then you showed us that when you fed thousands with only five loaves of bread and two fish (Matthew 14:19-21).

When I think about Sartu, God, I'm aware again of how much you have given me. You've blessed me to be a blessing. I pray for Sartu and her family to be safe and happy and filled with your Holy Spirit.

## A Rainy Day

Lord, there's nothing like a sweet spring rain to clean the air, refresh the landscape, and wash the streets. I also like rainy days for staying indoors so I can focus on a home or work project, spend time reading, or cook something special. I remember this little nursery rhyme: "Rain, rain, go away, come again another day." As a child I echoed this chant, but not anymore. I am grateful that you replenish our water supply for drinking, growing crops, swimming, boating, and fishing. All that we need your hand has provided just as the Thomas Chisholm hymn "Great Is Thy Faithfulness" reminds us.

# A New Store

I heard it yesterday. A new, large-scale variety store is opening not far from home. I can already imagine the well-stocked shelves, the shiny tile floor, the bright lights overhead illuminating all the latest merchandise. The manager is holding an open house tomorrow night, including drinks and refreshments and a tour of the facility.

Every new opening holds the promise of good things to come, Lord. But the excitement and newness eventually wear off, or the place loses money and closes, or a newer, better operation opens nearby. But with you, God, your mercies are new every morning (Lamentations 3:22-23 NCV). I count on that as I depend on you to guide me and guard me in everything I think, say, and do.

# Just a Handful

At the grocery store I walked down the aisle that displayed nuts and nut butters. I spotted a new item called "Just a Handful." Individual, large plastic bags contained a dozen or so smaller bags filled with almonds, or cashews, or a nut and cranberry mix. *What a good idea,* I thought. *I can keep one or two in my purse or car when I'm on the run between meals.* Everyone can use a little something to nibble on.

Then my mind wandered to the Bible and how you, Lord, provide bits of wisdom to nibble on when my spirit lags. The bite-sized verses in the books of Psalms and Proverbs are perfect spiritual pick-me-ups.

> *For the LORD gives wisdom; from his mouth come knowledge and understanding* (Proverbs 2:6).

> *Give thanks to the LORD, for he is good; his love endures forever* (Psalm 107:1).

## A Message from Heaven

O Lord, who'd have thought years ago that I'd be thanking you for something called "email"? I couldn't have imagined it, and yet here I am today, like millions of other people, relying on it for contact with people all over the world. A few clicks of the keys or mouse and a message, short or long, sails into cyberspace within seconds.

Today a woman wrote to me about her depression and worry over a family member. She asked for prayer support. I was able to respond immediately with a note from my heart just for her. I felt like an angel dispatching a message from heaven to someone in need. And when the situation is reversed, I receive the same comfort and hope from another "angel." So thank you, dear Lord, for the gift of communication that comes in many forms—cards, notes, letters, and email.

## Pretty Toes

Lord, is it vain to spend money on a pedicure? My faithful feet work so hard for me every day. I remember reading on the Internet that a person living until age 80 will have walked approximately 108,131 miles. Soaking my feet in warm, sudsy water, receiving a massage, and then picking out a pretty polish for my toenails seems the least I can do for them. Are you smiling at my silly question? I know you want me to take care of myself. You gave me eyes, and ears, and hands, and feet to use for your glory so I guess a pedicure is not out of line. Thank you, dear God.

# Dusting Photographs

It's time for a good spring-cleaning—the kind that includes more than merely dusting photographs. But one of my favorite tasks is doing just that! I like to linger over each one as I run a cloth around the frame and across the glass. How can so many years have passed since my girls (now mothers themselves) posed on the balance beam or my son stood ready with his tennis racket for a competitive match?

And what about me? Did I really have dark brown hair at one time? And whatever made me choose that navy blue dress with a white collar? I guess it was in style then or I wouldn't have bought it. One of my favorite pictures is of my sister, June, and me in matching flower-print dresses when we were three and six years old respectively, posed just so on a bench in the photographer's studio. Both of us are looking a bit serious for our ages. How sweet and innocent we were back then.

Thank you, Lord, for the science of photography. Capturing moments in time and saving them to enjoy over and over is such a wonderful gift. As I pick up and dust each picture I'm reminded of the days of my life and those of my children. I treasure each one.

# Pancakes

I remember taking one of our grandsons to House of Pancakes for his birthday one year. He ordered the chocolate chip stack, my husband chose blueberry, and true to my fitness convictions, I selected "Harvest Grain 'n Nut." We lathered our pancakes with fresh butter and warm maple syrup. I began thinking about you, Lord, and your generosity to our family.

As I watched us dive in and consume our food, I was touched by how much love we shared. Sometimes we show it with a hug, or kiss, or by enjoying a story with grandchildren perched on our laps, or sharing a Bible verse uttered at just the right moment, or, especially important, with three little words that say it all: "I love you."

We finished our breakfast, pushed our plates to the side, and talked a few more minutes before heading home. It was a wonderful time together—relaxed and happy. As you feed our bodies, God, you also nourish our souls if we open ourselves to you and receive your everlasting food. Jesus said, *"I am the living bread that came down from heaven. Whoever eats this bread will live forever"* (John 6:51). Thank you, Lord Jesus.

## A New Spring Outfit

It gives me such a lift, Lord, to buy a new outfit for a special occasion. I know I could settle for something already hanging in my closet, but sometimes I want to splurge. That doesn't mean spending money we don't have. The item could be on sale and practical enough to wear again and again. I never have been a person to go overboard, buying clothes just for the sake of buying them. But I enjoy slipping into a new pair of pants and a pretty blouse or jacket. Thank you for clothes, shoes, makeup, and jewelry. May I honor you most of all with my appearance.

## New Buds

O Lord, how I love the spring. Winter has passed and the promise of new beginnings is in the air and in my garden. I see the trees leafing out, small buds opening on the gardenia and azalea bushes, tiny insects skittering across the earth, and finches bobbing in and out of the birdbath.

I feel the renewal within myself as well. I am filled with hope and the promise of things to come. At last I can spend time in the yard, sitting at our picnic table under the large umbrella and reading or just relaxing and thinking. Thank you for that privilege and for the fresh thoughts you give me that fuel my prayer life and my writing. I'm never at a loss for words or ideas. I scoop them up like water from a stream, and there is always more. Your provision never runs out. I praise you for that and more.

## Can't or Won't Fix It?

"Can you fix the screen door?" I asked my husband. It was a beautiful spring day, and I wanted to open the main door and let in the warm breeze. But the knob on the screen door had broken off in my hand.

"All set!" he called moments later as he put away his tools and washed his hands in the kitchen sink.

"You're my hero!" I said and planted a kiss on his cheek.

Lord, if only all fix-it jobs were as easy as this one. A little twist here and there and everything works to my satisfaction. But life's not like that, and you know it better than I do. I not only want doors, and windows, and furniture, and bicycles, and cars fixed when something goes wrong, I want to *fix* the people in my life who drive me up the wall.

But I can't. My husband can't. And sometimes it seems that even you, God, can't. When that happens I freak out. I've always counted on you to be the supreme fix-it person. But then I get back into your Word and learn again that people have free will. You want to restore their spirits and bodies and draw them into a relationship with you, but you won't force or insist. You invite and then it's up to them to respond. When we are weary and heavily burdened, you promise rest and restoration. You are the only fix that lasts.

# Daffodils

Lord, for me springtime means daffodils. I pick up a small bunch each week at the grocery store for 99 cents. They're not much to look at sitting in a plain bucket without water at the end of the checkout counter. One could easily mistake the five or six flowers with their long, green stalks and white heads hidden in a pale sheath for a bunch of green onions bound together with a rubber band. But when I take them home and open up the wrapper, surprise! They're as beautiful as any rose—at least to me. I plunge them into a vase of water, and they open up into a golden bouquet that lasts an entire week.

I can't be sad or mad around daffodils. I can only be glad. They remind me of the true joy and pleasure of simply *being*. There is nothing for a "daffy" to do except *be*. Yet this quiet beauty speaks to me every morning and spills sunshine across my day, reminding me to bloom where I'm planted, be expectant and thankful for the gift of life—however many days I have left, and express my true self regardless of my surroundings or circumstances.

Like the lilies of the field, daffodils do not labor or spin. They simply *are*, and yet you, their heavenly Father and mine, cares for them and for me (Matthew 6:28-30).

# Celebration of Love

Ah, married life, dear God. It's not for wimps! There are so many ups and downs and turn arounds. How does any couple make it over the long haul? I wanted to know so I asked four women who'd been married 50 years or more, and they told me the truth straight up.

"I remember how God has proven himself worthy and faithful in the past," said Corinne. "Whenever we face difficulties, we stop and remember how God has taken care of us in the past. He's been with us through difficulties again and again. He's proven himself worthy."

"I stay open-minded and keep a sense of humor," Joan said. "I've had to learn to adapt and laugh at mistakes, smile at misunderstandings, and chuckle at misdeeds—especially when neither of us meant to hurt the other."

B.J. shared, "I gave up my right to be right. I learned the importance of that the hard way. I watched my mother-in-law press her 'rights' with my father-in-law while they were living with us." Right then and there B.J. changed direction. When she looked at her husband with new eyes, she said, "I saw what a precious person he is." That insight changed their relationship. "I now see that most marital problems really have very little to do with one's spouse. We get upset because we think *our* way of doing things is the *right* way or the *only* way. But it's not. The other person has his or her way, and it's as valid as ours."

"I'm committed because I desire to be," said Mabel. "That probably doesn't sound like a very profound answer, but it's true for me. I *want* to be committed to my husband." She remained positive in her outlook until the day he died. "When you love someone, you just keep going," Mabel added. "You don't stop loving him because there are changes. I take each day as it comes and do what's needed."

God, thank you for these wise women and their wise words. Here I go to love my husband—one day at a time and with your help.

## Serenity

Lord, I'm looking at the little ceramic bird on my desk as I write to you today. The words "God, grant me serenity" are written across its belly. I've placed the little guy in a conspicuous place so I can't miss his message. Serenity is something I want and need each day. And you are the only one who can guarantee it! For so long I looked to others to offer me the love and peace and loyalty I longed for. It's taken many years to come to this place of knowing that only *you* can grant it. Best of all, I know you *will*. All I have to do is ask. So today, dear God, please grant me serenity and allow me to be an example of this gift in the lives of others so they too will turn to you for peace.

## Sock It to 'Em

An elderly friend told me he discovered one morning that he was wearing two different-colored socks. How embarrassing, Lord, especially when a male acquaintance called it to his attention before he saw it for himself. At first he didn't know how to respond. He was afraid of being brought down in front of the younger guys who were heading to the golf course with him. But then, as one of them swung his club high in the air, *his* socks were in plain sight of everyone standing around him—one gray and one blue! And he was only 45 years of age. My friend had a good laugh and decided that being colorful is more important than being perfect.

## Lightly Salted

Lord, I'm thinking about the night my hiking friends and I ended our day with a few hours of conversation around the campfire. Someone passed a box of crackers. I noticed the label read "Lightly Salted." I smiled, thinking this might be a reminder from you to sprinkle salt lightly on those I meet and touch so they will not turn away but, instead, will "taste and see" that you are good (Psalm 34:8). May this be true of me today and every day. Thank you for reminders, nudges, and even shoves when need be. I want to walk with you and draw others to you and your path.

## Speaking Truth

Lord, I remember a speaker talking about the importance of being a light for others by the way we talk and behave. She realized during a crisis at the company where she works that she was opting for comfort instead of integrity. She was more focused on what her employees thought of her than what she thought of them. It became clear that she didn't think much of anyone but herself.

When her business took a dive without warning, she suddenly saw that she'd hidden her true light under a bowl of pride and self-will. In so doing, everyone in the company lost sight of the way to go. After the loss of three significant family members within two years, this woman returned to you and the Bible, with the help of someone who saw her pain. Her company, she acknowledges, is now a place of truth where all of them work together, own up to their mistakes, and do work that is suited to their talents.

I can learn from her experience, dear God. How often do I hide my light because I don't like confrontation? Instead, I need to raise it high to illuminate the truth that you set people free. Help me change, Lord!

## Never Too Late

Thank you, Lord, that it's never too late to dream a new dream, to start a new job, to repair an injured relationship, to make a new friend, to draw closer to you. Whatever we need, you provide—and more. I'm excited that even in my later years I can write a new book, prepare a fresh presentation, redo my website, and begin a blog. I don't have to flop into a rocking chair and watch life from my window. I can go outside and be part of the scene. It ain't over until you call me home!

## One Spring Day

How blessed I am to have had so many wonderful mentors and teachers in my life. I remember one spring day when a woman came into my life with words of wisdom that propelled me forward in my walk with you. She's with you in heaven now, but I had the privilege of drawing on her wisdom for nearly 30 years.

Thank you, God, for other loving and positive influences, as well. My kindergarten teacher who taught me about you, my fourth-grade teacher who encouraged me in my writing, my first mentor after I became a Christian, my husband, my sponsor in my recovery group, my two prayer partners, my writing instructors and editors and literary agents. What a privilege to learn from those who have gone before me. I want to do the same for the people I'm connected to. Help me, God, to remember that others are watching me, evaluating me, judging me. May I be a worthy example by pointing to you in all ways.

## Giant Landfill

That Wednesday morning years ago, dear Lord, you knew my life was a giant landfill. Everywhere I looked were bags of trash. Finances. Career. Marriage. Family relationships. Nothing worked well anymore. I'm so glad I was able to escape for a day of hiking with my friends. Thank you for that. It was such a blessing. I knew then, as I have many times since, that a good workout was just what I needed to gain some healthy perspective. But after the first hour on the trail, I could barely stand up. The rough patch of road went up and down like a roller coaster, and we lost ground almost as quickly as we gained it. "Not sure I can go on!" I called to my friends. Others agreed.

Then Hal, one of the stronger hikers, charged ahead. From a distance, he shouted, "Come on! You've got to see this view." I plowed ahead, inspired by his enthusiasm and a bit curious too. What a sight it was. Bountiful gifts as far as my eyes could see. Beautiful peaks poked above the clouds, tall trees and flowering shrubs dotted the hillsides, and small lakes and streams sparkled in the sun. Hal was right. And to think I almost missed these gifts because I was so weary and heavy-laden. I came home that day a different person, ready to face my problems with a new and higher point of view. How I thank you, Lord, for helping me to keep going—even when the going was rough. There's always a treasure at the end of the road.

## Snowballs in Spring

Lord, I just came from the hair salon. Of the five women in the shop, four had been divorced, including me. One was sharing freely about her ex-husband and what a bum he is. "But he'll pay the price someday," she said. "They always do. Just wait." I heard a trickle of delight in her voice. I smiled, thinking the same thing about my ex—even though it's been more than 30 years since we parted.

At first I kept quiet, but then I found myself joining the fray. This one said one thing and that one another. Pretty soon I added my two cents worth about how it took nearly three decades for me to see any justice in my situation. What a terrible thing to say, I suddenly realized. Who am I to decide when and where and what justice is for this man? He's in *your* hands, Lord, not mine.

I married the guy, so I must have seen something worthwhile at the time or I'd never have said yes. I'm feeling ashamed right now, and I ask your forgiveness, Lord. I'm no saint. I have my own list of sins to contemplate. That will keep me plenty busy for the rest of my life. Please keep me from throwing snowballs at my ex just because others are doing so at theirs. Instead, remind me to pray for those who are tossing and those who are the targets.

## Breast Friends

Gosh, Lord, so many women I know are being diagnosed with breast cancer. At least three in the last few months. So far I've escaped, and I'm so grateful even though I don't know what tomorrow may bring. I pray for these friends, and ask you to keep their spirits up, their hearts full of love for you, their minds focused on your promise never to leave or forsake them. And thank you for the marvels of modern medicine that produce such good results if the cancer is caught early. May each of these women—and thousands more—draw a little closer to you as they undergo treatment and move into recovery.

# Picture Perfect

It's a beautiful spring day, and our neighbor stopped by to take our photograph in the yard near our flowerbed. He's pretty handy with a camera, but I didn't prepare for his visit so I'm wearing an old striped shirt and my hair isn't the way I'd like it to be. Oh well, it's kind of him to think of us. Maybe he's just practicing with his new equipment. Maybe I look fine the way I am. I'm too fussy about my appearance these days, aware of every line and wrinkle that I can no longer hide. Let's face it, I'm old. There's only so much I can do with what I have. Perhaps it's time to don a coat of humility and just say thanks instead of worrying about how I look to others—including the camera.

God, old age is creeping up my legs, down my arms, and across my face. I can't catch it, so I can't stop it. I guess the best thing to do is accept it with gratitude—since I'm actually very blessed to have made it this far and still be in good health and sound mind. Hey, Lord, I just excused myself from the pity party! I feel good about myself now—even my looks. In fact, as I pause to look in the mirror, I see that I'm picture perfect in your eyes.

# What's Next?

Lord, someone once told me it's better that we don't know what's next in our lives because we might not be able to stand it. I guess if I were to win a million dollars, or find out I could sail to Hawaii with all expenses paid, or that my sister would be cured of her condition—then I'd like knowing what's next.

But if I were to hear that my husband is going to die soon, or my daughter will be moving to a new city, or that my son lost his business, or that I will break a leg, I'd rather not know what's next. In fact, regardless of whether the future holds challenges or victories or a little of each, I think I'm happier not knowing. I'd rather entrust all my "nexts" to you. You know the right time and place for such events to occur, and you know how much I can stand or not stand knowing ahead of time.

You say in your Word that you will never give me too much or too little, but only what I can handle by your grace. Thank you for that. I rest now in the knowledge that *all* things—good and bad, disappointing and exciting—will work together for good because you love me and I love and follow you.

## A Spring in My Step

It's springtime, and I feel a spring in my step. Is that corny or is it a sign that I feel better at this time of year than at any other time? I have to admit that I'm always hopeful and happy and forward-thinking when the weather warms up, the buds leaf out on the trees, and flower bulbs poke their heads above the soil. "Is it time yet?" they seem to ask.

"Yes, yes it is!" I reply. "Come on up. It's delightful." With flowers and weeds bursting forth in the hot sunshine, there is more work to do in the garden. But I don't mind. It's good for me to put my gloved hands in the soil, refill the birdbath, and pluck a pretty rose for the vase on the dining room table.

Lord, I look forward to hiking in the forest, along the shore, and across meadows. The songs of the birds will lead me! They swoop and stop and then take off again, sometimes to join their feathered friends on a telephone line along Main Street in town. They appear as optimistic as I am, so I join in by humming my own tune. Yes, God, spring is a lovely time of year filled with the promise of things to come and the sweet peace that only your Spirit can convey. I surely do have a spring in my step today!

## Hold Me Tight, Lord

I had a bad dream last night, dear God. I don't even remember the details now—only that it was scary at the time. I think I lost my purse or my keys or my cell phone. I'm not sure, but I was frantic. These items have become so much a part of me that I don't dare misplace them. But now that I'm awake and can see and touch my purse and keys and phone, I'm relaxed. I'm not at risk anymore—at least for the moment.

I guess what I need right now is a big hug, Lord. Please hold me tight and remind me that you are always here for me whether I'm awake or asleep, whether I'm coasting along or in a conflict. Help me remember that I have nothing to worry about. Like the lilies of the field and the birds of the air in springtime, all of my needs are met in you. And if you care for the sweet flowers and winged friends who may be here today and gone tomorrow, how much more do you care for me, your child! Thank you for being my Father God.

## Cats and Weeds

Oh no! Not another day of sweeping bark and leaves scattered by our neighbor's cat. He doesn't dare tear up our flowerbed during the day. He seems to prefer the stealth of night—when few people will see him. Is he mad at us, God, for chasing him and showing our impatience with loud voices? Or is he a creature, like so many others, who is ignored and avoided when times are tough? Maybe all he wants is a little attention, and he'll take it however he can get it—even if it means resorting to bad behavior.

And then there are the weeds that pop up the moment spring arrives. They want to be seen too, I guess, so they intrude on the flower garden and push themselves up through open spaces between the flagstones. I picked some today and tossed them into a bucket…

but then I felt a little remorse. After all, they are your creation too. Maybe it's best if I surrender to the way things are. Weeds and cats come and go. They are part of nature, and all of nature belongs to you.

## A Time to Mourn

A friend of mine died within the last couple of weeks. I like knowing she is with you, Lord, but I will miss her at conferences and conventions. Most of all I'll miss her prayers. This woman knew how to pray and how to encourage. All through her cancer treatment she kept on going—praying, sharing, teaching—even on days when her energy flagged and her strength petered out. I can learn from her example. Thank you for my friend who is now with you.

## All Is Well

I attended a prayer group with my sister and was inspired to hear the leader conclude the evening with the famous words written in the fourteenth century by Dame Julian of Norwich, one of the most important Christian mystics:

> All shall be well,
> And all shall be well,
> And all manner of things shall be well.

I remembered as I listened, Lord, that this quotation is engraved on a silver candle holder a friend gave my husband and me as a housewarming gift. I focused on the words for a moment or two and found comfort in the hope and promise they offer. No matter what we've faced in the past, are facing now, or will face in the future, "all shall be well" when we walk with you. Even if we don't understand why things happen as they do, we can rest in the knowledge that you know and will use these experiences for good.

When I live in the moment instead of escaping to the future or dwelling on the past, I see indeed that all is well, and all shall be well—in all manner of things.

## Falling Together

Lord, today I'm thinking about my dad when he lost his job at age 60—fired just like that when a large conglomerate purchased the firm he worked for. He had no special training and hadn't even finished high school. At 15 he'd quit school and went to work to help support his large family.

It wasn't easy finding new work at an age when many people were about to retire, but he had to do something fast. He had a wife and children to take care of. I remember Dad combing the pages of the *Wall Street Journal* looking for small businesses that were available to buy or sell. He hoped to put owners and buyers together. Within three years he was not only established in this new field of business mergers, but he earned more money in commissions than he'd ever earned in his previous career. God, you blessed him beyond anything he envisioned.

I asked him how he kept his wits and his health during that time of great stress. "I leaned on Jesus," he said. "He's a good friend to have." My father gave all the glory to you, Lord, the One he knew as the author and finisher of his life and work.

Dad's example cast a light on my path. When my life was about to fall apart after a divorce, I looked to Dad and you, and "fell together" instead. Thank you for the gift of my father on earth and of you, my Father in heaven.

## Traffic Jam

Lord, thank you for helping me become a safe driver. Instead of being impatient with people who dart in and out of lanes around me or faulting myself for not paying closer attention to such drivers, I've decided to pray. What an experience it has been! I whisper a prayer of protection for myself as well as everyone I encounter on city streets and freeways. It's made all the difference, especially during spring break from school and around the holidays when traffic is intense.

As I pray, I actually feel alert rather than distracted. My heart and mind are in the right place—full of good will instead of judgment and annoyance. I'm also reminded of this encouraging verse from your Word: *"If it is possible, as far as it depends on you, live at peace with everyone"* (Romans 12:18).

Focusing on you while driving in traffic is something I now look forward to each day as I get into my car. And I hope my prayers will help bring peace and calm to other drivers and passengers, as well as to myself.

## Job Shortage

The job shortage is disheartening, Lord, especially for young men and teens. The *Wall Street Journal* said this group of job hunters remains unemployed, on average, for 32 months before finding meaningful work. I know how it is. One of my grandsons falls into this group. But when I think about such challenges, I'm reminded to pray for every one of us because we never know what might happen when we least expect it.

On the other hand, our pastor said during a sermon that interruptions and inconveniences can become blessings in disguise. So true! I've experienced this countless times. I come begging you to release me from pain, sorrow, fear, and worry, and before I know it the very thing I dread turns into a good thing in my life—something that leads to a greener pasture.

Job seekers may not know what employment will come their way, but they can know what you have in mind for them. You tell us exactly what not to do: *"Don't worry about these things, saying, 'What will we eat? What will we drink? What will we wear?' These things dominate the thoughts of unbelievers, but your heavenly Father already knows all your needs"* (Matthew 6:31-32 NLT).

We can rest knowing that we'll never be abandoned by you. One way or the other, oftentimes in unexpected ways, *you* will provide. Take care of job hunters today, Lord. Bring them a blessing in disguise.

## What's New?

When I flip on the evening news, dear God, I'm tempted to turn it off almost immediately because there's so much bad stuff. But even as I watch and listen, I realize I'm finding your presence there. I don't have to be tuned to a religious channel to experience you. News—whether good or bad—does involve you, the Creator of the universe, because you care about your people and creation and what happens. War, murder, theft, and other criminal activity doesn't escape your notice. Sometimes it's hard to understand your love for the perpetrators as well as the victims. Your Word says, *"God so loved the world, that He gave His only begotten Son, that whoever believes in Him shall not perish, but have eternal life"* (John 3:16). What a powerful piece of good news this is. Your Son, Jesus Christ, is ready to forgive, to restore, to assure *anyone* who asks for it that he or she can turn away from evil and live a clean and grace-filled life through Jesus. And for those who have been victimized by others, you promise to set them free of fear, hurt, and resentment. How amazing is your grace, dear God.

## The Tax Man Cometh

Lord, here we go again. Spring not only brings showers and flowers but taxes too. I started putting together my work-related income and expense documents last week. It took much longer than I anticipated even though I keep good records. At first I felt agitated, as I'm sure you know. I had to dig a little deeper than usual to find some items, and I needed to contact a few people for forms that had not yet arrived. As soon as I felt my pulse rise, I took a deep breath and said a quick, "Help, Lord!"

Within seconds I felt my shoulders relax, my mind clear, and my spirit rest in you. I moved on to fill in the information I did have and felt a surge of gratitude that I had made enough income to even pay taxes. I want to do my part in keeping our highways repaired, our schools running, our teachers and government workers paid, and our armed forces protecting our freedom. Paying taxes also means that my work is thriving, and I can count on making a living at what I love to do. Hey, Lord, I feel better already—just getting all this off my chest.

As former associate justice of the U.S. Supreme Court Oliver Wendell Holmes, Jr. put it: "I like to pay taxes. With them I buy civilization." And as Paul advises in his letter to the Christians in Rome: *"Give to everyone what you owe them: If you owe taxes, pay taxes; if revenue, then revenue; if respect, then respect; if honor, then honor"* (Romans 13:7). Will do! Thank you, God.

## Easter Surprise

Sunlight streamed through my bedroom window and poked me in the eyes one Sunday morning in April, 1948. "Wake up. It's Easter!" I called to my sister.

She popped up and rubbed the sleep from her eyes. I remember how we bounded down the stairs to the kitchen and opened the refrigerator. Sure enough, true to his custom, Dad had placed three beautiful carnation corsages on the top shelf—one for Mom, one for my sister, and one for me.

Lord, what a lovely memory this is! I'm thinking about the times when we stepped into our pretty spring dresses, lacy socks, and patent leather slippers. At that time of my life, Easter was all about clothes, candy, Easter eggs, and the beautiful baskets Mom filled with goodies.

It wasn't until decades later that, without warning, my life turned inside out like an umbrella in a rainstorm. My husband left our family. I was soon alone, divorced, and scared out of my mind at what lay ahead.

I needed a *Savior*, which you knew well. And into my life you came, dear Jesus. The one I had read about, sang about, learned about, but never really *knew* until you came alive through the pages of Scripture and the shared experiences of caring people in a Bible study I attended as a guest of a new friend.

Easter *that* year—more than 30 years after the Easter morn I remembered from 1948—was the first time I walked in the only new garments that matter. I was clothed in your righteousness, released from sin, restored in spirit, and recognized as a friend of yours, my almighty God. I'm so glad you sent your Son, Jesus, who said:

*I am the resurrection and the life. The one who believes in me will live, even though they die; and whoever lives by believing in me will never die* (John 11:25-26).

Receiving your forgiveness, love, and grace that year, dear God, changed my life forever. Oh how I thank you!

## New Shoes

Thank you, God, for the pair of sturdy-but-attractive sandals I found for my camping trip. I needed something to slip in and out of easily as I trotted around the campsite before and after our daily treks. When I walked into the local department store and saw exactly what I was looking for in the women's shoe department—and on sale!—I knew you were in this with me. Thank you. This find made my day. Not only did you provide what I needed, but you did so within my budget.

It's little reminders like this that increase my faith each day. Yes, reading the Bible is important, as is saying daily prayers and being attentive to your teachings, but when you show up in small, surprising ways—like when I'm buying a pair of shoes, or looking for just the right outfit for a wedding, or seeking the perfect gift for a loved one's birthday—well, that really brings a smile to my face and a boost to my faith. Then I know again, without a doubt, that you are with me in the mundane and the meaningful. You're with me, period. All I have to do is talk to you, confide in you, and trust you to do for me what I can't do for myself. Thank you, Lord.

## Behind Bars

Lord, it's been a blessing to be part of my friend's prison ministry by corresponding with inmates. I've never visited a prisoner before, but I've had a desire to encourage women to trust in you. These women are incarcerated for drugs, theft, and other criminal activities. I want them to know your love and to offer them the hope they can find in you no matter where they are or what they've done.

This experience has been life changing for me. I write to mothers and grandmothers who are locked up physically and spiritually. We're doing a Bible study together, which they receive free of charge.

They can complete it over several months, and then they send their answers to me. I treasure the opportunity to read their responses to each lesson and reply to their comments with a Scripture verse or a few words of support.

Sometimes I cry, other times I smile as I see the gradual changes that come about in the lives of these women I write to. They seem to experience you in a way that many on the "outside" never do. Maybe it's because they have nothing—no money, clothing, or possessions they can call their own at this point in time. They are wards of the state and live by prison rules and regulations 24/7.

I thank you, God, for making your presence known to them in small and big ways, including through your Word and through the friendship of correspondents like me. I feel deeply blessed to interact with these women and see how the seeds of love and comfort can blossom into a relationship with you that surpasses their expectations and understanding.

## A Breath of Springtime

The hills are alive today, dear Lord, with sunlight streaming down, birds flitting from branch to branch, and laughter and chatter filling the air among my hiking pals. As we trek up and down the trails in the foothills above our little farming community, I'm aware of encountering the peace and serenity I crave. It's here in nature, especially in springtime, in this place you created for us to enjoy. I inhale. Exhale. Inhale. Exhale. Breathing deeply I feel my head clear, my eyes brighten, and my emotions even out. Everything I want and need, you provide, Lord. I am so grateful.

When my friends and I come to the end of our hike, we'll pack our gear into our cars and head down the hill to the Gizdich Ranch for apple or blueberry or olallieberry pie with ice cream on top. *Yum!* As I savor the last forkful, I will again think of you, dear Lord. Even a slice of berry pie starts with the seeds you provided by your gracious hand, planted in the bountiful ground you created, and nourished by the water, sunlight, and nutrients you send.

## Discount Day

Saturday is discount day in many stores near my home. Lord, as other shoppers and I browse for great bargains on clothes, shoes, kitchen gadgets, tools, toys, and so much more, my thoughts turn to you. Certainly in former days I didn't associate you with such an activity. Not at all. I was into shopping, not conversing with you. Now I associate you with everything. And last week you came to mind when I noticed spring sale signs were posted all over town.

I stepped back a few paces and simply observed the people selling and the men, women, and children coming and going. It made me smile. Neighbors were chatting comfortably and enjoying glasses of lemonade or free cups of coffee at the curb. They visited while fingering items and checking their wallets or purses for the money to purchase what they wanted. Vendors earned money, and buyers took home the things that caught their eye.

I left the shopping center with a smile on my face and a lilt in my heart. You show up, dear God, in the most unexpected places and in unpredictable ways. A toddler's face when his mom hands him a toy, a dad's reassuring arm around his daughter who is holding a game, a teen laughing and chatting as she debates whether to part with her hard-earned dollars. You are among us always—your presence assured even in the mundane. What a comfort that is.

# Palm Trees

Thank you for the gift of graceful palm trees, dear Lord. I'm tickled at how easy it is to think of you when I see these stately specimens. They reflect your power and how it cannot be swayed by the storms of life. I've watched palms bend almost to the point of touching the ground. But when the wind stops, they bounce back to their original upright positions. How creative of you to give them such flexibility.

I know the same can be true of me when I trust you completely. I love this reference to palms in your Word: *"The righteous will flourish like a palm tree"* (Psalm 92:12). You knew I'd experience tough times, relationship challenges, sickness, and financial stresses. When I turn to you in prayer, the winds of worry, and fear, and darkness stop blowing. I stand straight again—even stronger than before.

# Promises! Promises!

Lord, I'm thinking of the warm spring evening my husband lay sprawled on the sofa with his tie loosened and his feet propped on the coffee table. The television hummed in the background. The newspaper was in a pile on the floor. A bowl of half-finished popcorn was perched on his abdomen, rising and falling with each breath he took. It was a sight I'd grown accustomed to over the years, but not one I liked at all. I wanted to shake Charles awake and tear into him with my frustration.

Our wonderful periods of togetherness and intimacy were too often followed by these sudden gaps in our communication. Only you, Lord, could snatch us from the abyss we were hovering over. And only you could transform the way I responded to my husband. And you did!

Unexpectedly and wonderfully, you redeemed our lives through a marriage study group. Slowly, over time, we grew close again, finding you when we kept our promises to one another and met with other couples to share our hearts and listen to the challenges they faced. Keeping our promises to one another is not nearly the challenge it once was because now we are in fellowship each day with you, Jesus, the greatest Promise Keeper of all. *"[The Lord] remembered his covenant forever, the word which He commanded to a thousand generations"* (Psalm 105:8 NASB).

## By Faith—Not Sight

As I look back on my life, I did just the opposite of what the apostle Paul taught in the Bible: *"We walk by faith, not by sight"* (2 Corinthians 5:7 NASB). Finding God by faith and not by sight took me by surprise when, at age 42, I finally committed my life to you. I'd lived by sight for so long. All my choices and decisions were based on what I felt, what I noticed, what I heard, and what I saw in the world. I held my own point of view in high regard, as you well know.

But when a financial crisis knocked me down one spring day, I lay there as still as a stone. I had no resources, no help, no answers—until a counselor friend asked me a disturbing question: "How are you and God getting along?" *What kind of a question is that?* I wondered. I hadn't even thought about you, Lord, except when I said a casual thank you before a meal. But my friend's question wouldn't let go of me. It started a journey that led me to your teachings, your promises, your friendship—and to the knowledge that to walk with you is to live by faith, not by sight.

# SUMMER

*Now learn this lesson from the fig tree:*
*As soon as its twigs get tender and its leaves come out,*
*you know that summer is near.*

Matthew 24:32

---

*"All in all, it was a never-to-be-forgotten summer—*
*one of those summers which come seldom into any life,*
*but leave a rich heritage of beautiful*
*memories in their going."*

L.M. Montgomery

# Hurt Feelings

"You said what?" my husband demanded as he stormed into our home office and glared at me with hurt and anger. My pulse jumped and my heart turned to mush. What had I said? I didn't recall. But he did. And, Lord, certainly you knew. For a guy who half the time can't remember his best friend's name or that of our grandchild in another city, Charles had no problem letting me know that what I'd said earlier to someone else had wounded him.

My first thought was to defend myself. I could explain if he'd just let me. But then you, my gentle Lord, tapped me on the shoulder and whispered, "Hear his feelings." You were right, of course. I backpedaled and suddenly the words came. "I see that I really hurt you. I'm so sorry. I meant to be playful. How thoughtless of me. Please forgive me."

"Okay," he said, and then took a deep breath.

We were friends again, and I was relieved. Lord, if only I'd heed your cues more often.

# A Good Phone Call

My eldest daughter called today, and we had a good chat and a good laugh. She's over 50 now, so her kids are almost grown up. She's going through some of the same challenges I faced when I was her age and she was their age. You know the ones, Lord. Kids driving parents crazy, doors slamming, teens in and out with friends to feed, complaints about home cooking, the need to lean on parents when things get tough. My daughter chuckled when she remembered that she leaned on me the same way—and still does at times.

Lord, I like to be needed, but I also know things work out best when we lean on your understanding, not our own. Thank you for my son and daughters, for the words and laughter we share, and for the ability to end every conversation and email with an "I love you" because of your great love. Let me never close a talk with you, Lord, without doing the same. "I love you."

## Worry Free

I read an article this week in the newspaper about letting anxiety work *for* me instead of against me. Now there's a concept I can get behind, Lord. I don't want to exhaust myself with worry and fear when you've made it clear that I am *not* to take on either one:

> *Do not be anxious about anything, but in every situation, by prayer and petition, with thanksgiving, present your requests to God. And the peace of God, which transcends all understanding, will guard your hearts and your minds in Christ Jesus* (Philippians 4:6-7).

Losing sleep over writing deadlines, the needs of my adult children, my husband's health, or whether we'll have enough money for our summer vacation doesn't solve any of those issues. But turning to you in rest and in trust puts them where they ought to be—in your hands. Thank you for always being here for me, dear God.

## Ouch!

Lord, please protect my grandchildren from the wiles of this world. They are so innocent. And yet we all have to learn, I guess, in our own ways. Last week my grandson was proud to tell me that he'd captured a bee. He held out his cupped hands in front of me. I warned him about getting stung, but he was certain it wouldn't happen to him. He and his friends had held bees hostage before and nothing bad had happened, he said. Then he went outside. Within seconds of uttering that assurance he ran back into the house screaming.

The bee got the best of him this time. Even as we comforted and reassured him, his mother and I bit back smiles at this step in learning to accept and follow advice. I doubt he'll be trying that prank on bees again anytime soon. He learned his lesson.

This incident made me think of how often I've toyed with misbehavior—a bit of disobedience here, a little gossip there and avoiding the inevitable consequences until I got stung. I inadvertently hurt a friend or wounded a neighbor or got caught speeding and had to pay a big fine. Lord, will I ever listen and get all the lessons you have for me without struggling? Or must I continually learn the hard way?

Today I watched the bees in my flowerbed and smiled as they went about their business. As long as I stay clear of them, they won't do me any harm. A lesson worth remembering. Thank you.

## Take a Hike!

Lord, I'm getting keyed up. Only three weeks till mid-July when my friend and I drive to the mountains for a week of camping and hiking with our all-gals group. Our leader is 80 years old this year, and the youngest among us is in her sixties. But on we go, carrying out our annual tradition. We're a bit slower than we used to be, and we don't scale the heights of past trips, but we do what we can. President Theodore Roosevelt once said, "Do what you can, with what you have, where you are." Yeah, Teddy, I'm with you on this. My friend and I have committed to going on this trek each year until we can't crawl around a tent anymore. "When that happens, we'll just stay in a nearby motel," she said. "But we're not giving up!" I agreed. We might be growing older, but we're not wimps. We can still hike—and we plan to do just that.

## Greener Grass

Lord, I've been wondering, "Is the grass sometimes greener on the other side of the street or is it my imagination because I sometimes feel dissatisfied with what's on my side?" I thought about this while on vacation in Ireland recently. I went out for a walk one afternoon alongside a pasture filled with sheep and lambs. I stopped when I saw one of the little ones climb through the slatted fence and wander over to the field on the opposite side of the road. He munched for quite some time, but after he'd had his fill he scampered back to where he'd come from, crawling through the fence to join the other babes.

I chuckled, wishing I could ask him if what he saw really had been better than what he'd had. I'll never know, but I did learn from his example. I'm like that more often than I care to admit. Would life be easier and greener if I had as much money as so-and-so, or if I wrote a bestseller that hit the *New York Times* list, or if I had the lovely complexion of the woman who works out next to me in the fitness class? Probably not.

When I come back to reality, I see that what I have, what I look like, and where I live is *perfect* for me because it is your design for my unique life. I calm down, settle into reality, and focus on the green grass in my pasture and following you, my shepherd.

## A Summer Wedding

Lord, how gracious you are to bring my nephew and his bride-to-be together at Braille school. I'm excited about their upcoming wedding. Corbb is an amazing young man. Born completely blind, he has already accomplished so much in his lifetime—independent studies abroad, a college degree from George Washington University, working for some noted politicians, and now setting up a home for life with his love.

I'm so impressed with his tenacity, his love for life, and his commitment to carry on despite the challenge of not being able to see. I keep thinking of this couple and how they'll never physically see each other's faces...or the wedding photos...or the gifts that will pour in.

This realization has made me even more grateful for the gift of sight and the good report I received when I had my health checkup a few weeks ago. But even with excellent vision, the apostle Paul reminds us that we all see through a glass darkly when we are on this side of heaven. Maybe my nephew and his fiancé see more than I do in a way I'll never understand. Thank you, Lord, for guiding each of us as we look to you for the help we need.

## Watermelon Days

"Two for $5" read the sign in the produce section of our local market. I couldn't pass up this great buy! Two sweet, round watermelons for such a price. I carried them to my basket and then home to include in a fruit salad for dinner. My husband was delighted when I served him a bowl filled with the juicy treats.

Watermelon takes me back to my childhood, Lord. A place I return to in my mind more often now that I'm growing older. Dad liked to sprinkle salt on his watermelon wedge. Grandpa wouldn't eat it because he thought it was about as tasteless as a glass of water. My sister and I dove in, devoured the chunks we were served, and spit out the seeds. What fun!

I've thanked you for a lot of things, God, but I doubt watermelon was ever on the list. So today I thank you for watermelon and strawberries and peaches and plums—favorite fruits from my early years...and in my later years too.

## Time-Out

Today, Lord, I'm thinking about when my kids were little. If I caught them misbehaving, I'd assign them a time-out. They hated it! They wanted to remain in the family room where all the action was. The same thing occurred in my daughter's household. On Sunday afternoons she and her husband needed a break from the noisy brood, so they gave their kids a one-hour time-out in their rooms. The moment the clock struck the hour they burst from their confinement ready to have fun. I imagine them camped out just inside their bedroom doors, wanting to be as close as possible to the exit when they were set free. I laugh when I think about it now.

At this stage of my life a time-out sounds divine. I tire of the normal routine—wake up, shower, eat breakfast, clean up the dishes, check the bank account, make a shopping list, go to the gym for a workout, visit with a friend, and then get to work on my latest book or article. I'd love it if someone shouted "Time-out!" to me…and then enforced it. I'm smiling as I realize that you have called to me over and over again through your Word to do just that!

> *Come to me, all you who are weary and burdened, and I will give you rest* (Matthew 11:28).

> *Come with me by yourselves to a quiet place and get some rest* (Mark 6:31).

> *In repentance and rest is your salvation, in quietness and trust is your strength* (Isaiah 30:15).

Got it, Lord! I'm taking a time-out right now.

## In One Room and Out the Other

Lord, I'm all too familiar with the expression "in one ear and out the other." I've been guilty on many counts of hearing and forgetting just like that. But lately, as I'm growing older, I'm creating my own variation of that saying. "In one room and out the other" is becoming the norm around our house. I walk into the office to make a note on my to-do list, forget what I wanted to write, so I move on to the kitchen. Then I head out the front door to get the newspaper, forgetting my plan to make oatmeal for breakfast. Oh dear!

Gettin' old can indeed be wearisome. But you know my situation better than I do, Lord. Today I'm turning my day over to you and trusting that when I enter a room with a goal in mind, you'll make it stick until I finish it. Thank you for helping me.

## Shoe Dog

I love my husband, Lord, quirks and all. My guy is an old "shoe dog," as the saying goes among shoe salespeople. He sold shoes at a department store while in high school, and after he "retired" at 60, he worked part-time and then fulltime selling men's shoes. My guy's worth his weight in loafers and tennies—lace-ups and slip-ons. He has more shoes than I do. Twenty-some pairs to date, a few of which are more than 20 years old. His shoes will definitely outlast him.

So what arrives in today's mail for Father's Day? A pair of Nikes from his daughter! They're a perfect fit in a lovely shade of gray with a touch of red. They're just right for casual wear. As he places them on the shelf in our closet, I scan his collection again. Lord, help me keep my sense of humor because my husband's footwear has reached twenty-one pairs and counting.

## Breakfast for a Good Cause

A neighbor came to the door just now selling tickets for a ham and eggs breakfast at a local restaurant to benefit the American Cancer Society. I don't feel like paying for breakfast out when I prefer eating at home. What should I do, Lord? Buy the tickets and don't go? Give up my desire to eat at home and go, telling myself it's for a good cause? Or wait and see how that day's going? I don't have to make a decision based on what someone else wants me to do. That tendency has been a fault of mine for as long as I can remember. I'm a people pleaser when I want to be a God pleaser. Thank you for reminding me.

## A Carriage Ride

Automobiles have been around since I was a baby, so I've never had to rely on horse-drawn vehicles for transportation. But I've always looked at them in movies and on the streets in big cities like New York with a desire to ride in one. I wanted to be taken down the road to the rhythmic clip-clop, clip-clop of a team of horses pulling a carriage or wagon. I got my chance while in Ireland. Charles and I took a nice, long, leisurely ride from Blarney to the Muckross House, where Queen Victoria and other dignitaries have stayed over the years. Eight of us took our places on the wooden planks that served as bench-style seats and listened as the driver entertained us with the history of the area.

I enjoyed the wind blowing through my hair, the lovely flowering plants, and the great trees standing along the road that ran through the forest. Thank you, God, for creating horses and for giving me my heart's desire—to ride in a horse-drawn wagon and pretend I was an Irish lass from long ago.

*Take delight in the Lord, and he will give you the desires of your heart* (Psalm 37:4).

# Prayer for the Suffering

Lord, on this beautiful summer day when I am well, happy, productive, and serene, I'm aware of those around me who are suffering—family members, friends, neighbors, and strangers. Health issues trouble young and old, insufficient finances worry some, while others have challenges in their relationships. People feel neglected, misunderstood, even angry, that things are not better between them and the ones they love. I understand these concerns because I've experienced them all at various times in my life. But today is not one of those times! I thank you, Lord, for the blessings I have, the lessons I've learned from the times I've suffered, and the reminder to pray each day for those who are having a tough time. Bless those who suffer. May they feel your love and experience your comfort.

# Polished to a "T"

Just now the doorbell rang. I'm not expecting anyone, and I sure hope no one has stopped by to chat. I'm trying to meet a writing deadline! I checked through the peephole. The man on the porch is my husband, eager to show me how beautiful and inviting the front door looks after he washed and polished it. He even gave our summer wreath a good dousing with the hose. What sweet gifts. This dear man keeps me in delightful surprises—from a single rose when I arrive home after a speaking engagement to a sparkling front door after a summer wind left dust in its wake.

Lord, you've given me a wonderful mate, an excellent partner in domestic affairs, and a loyal and generous spouse. How blessed I am. And knowing that he loves you best of all makes my heart sing. With you at the helm of his life he can't go wrong, and the benefit to me is another way in which you show me your love.

## MMOB

Lord, I remember as a child I was often told to MYOB, "mind your own business." I didn't like hearing that. I wanted to mind everyone's business but my own. I had such good ideas for how life would improve for my parents, siblings, and friends if they'd just listen to me. They rarely did. Instead they liked telling me how to run my affairs—from school to games, from sports to relationships. I want to break this lifelong habit of minding other people's business before it breaks me.

Today I'm a mother of three grown children and two stepchildren and grandmother to eight of my own grandchildren and four of my husband's. My days in charge are long over, but still I look into their lives and want to advise them how to experience happier, more orderly days. Do they want me to share this priceless information with them? Not really. At least not unless they ask, and right now only one has the ears to hear. Help me keep my lips zipped—unless I'm asked, of course. Remind me to MMOB, "mind my own business."

## A Tree and Me

Poet Joyce Kilmer (1886–1918) wrote these famous words: "Only God can make a tree." I thought about that yesterday while driving through the forest with my husband on a summer's day. Everywhere we looked trees abounded—giant redwoods, douglas firs, and ponderosa pines. Some have been in place for hundreds, maybe thousands of years. If blight destroys them, fire singes their bark, or winds take them down, they're powerless to help themselves. They are utterly dependent on you, God, for regeneration.

Not only are you the only one to make a tree, but only you could have made me. I'm your treasured creation too—one that your Son,

Jesus, died to save. Thank you that when the winds of temptation or the fires of sin sweep through my soul, you are here to rescue me and give me a chance to start anew.

## Prettiest One

"You're the prettiest one at the party," my husband declared as we sat under a warm, summer sun during a celebration of contributors to our city's symphony.

"Really?" I turned and looked him in the eye. I couldn't imagine that he thought I was more attractive than the brunette with the big straw hat, shapely legs, gorgeous tan, and bare arms without a wrinkle in sight. I didn't draw his attention to her. I figured what he didn't notice could stay that way. I certainly wasn't going to point him in the direction of my competition!

His words comforted my aging heart. For a moment I forgot that I wouldn't be caught dead wearing a short skirt that would expose the veins in my legs or a sleeveless blouse that would broadcast that my arms have seen better days.

But then I remembered that, like you, God, my husband doesn't look only at my outer appearance. He cares how I look within. He loves me for my soul and my mind—things that outshine my body and make me who I am. How blessed I am that the man I'm married to knows who I am and loves me anyway. And he still thinks I'm the prettiest woman around.

## Living Water

Dear Lord, as I grow older I'm making a point of drinking more water more often. It's good for my body and my mind. It clears my complexion, cleanses my system, and energizes me all day long. Why didn't I adopt this habit sooner? Because I got caught up in all the hoopla about fruit drinks and sodas and vitamin water. No more! I'm going with plain, fresh, clean water. This reminds me that on a spiritual level when I stick close to you—the Living Water—I will never thirst again! You quench all my desires that are not of you and grow the desires that are. So bottoms up, Lord! Here's to you, the One who cleanses, purifies, and refreshes my spirit day in and day out.

## Pants on Fire

I'm remembering, Lord, the funny playground taunt I heard as a kid: "Liar, liar, pants on fire." I never thought of myself as a liar back then. An exaggerator, maybe, but never a liar. But I realize that wasn't true. I don't make a habit of lying, but when I'm in a pickle I resort to twisting the truth a bit to suit myself. How embarrassing to admit it...but then you already know my weaknesses.

A neighbor invited me to meet for coffee to talk about her new business selling beauty products. It was the last thing I felt like doing. I didn't want to hear a long spiel, be asked to try the various tubes and bottles of this and that, or host a summer home party for my friends to promote her new enterprise. So why didn't I just admit it? Just say this sort of thing isn't for me? Why did I worry about hurting her feelings by declining, but then hurt her anyway by hemming and hawing? I'm sure she got the message from my lack of enthusiasm. Isn't withholding encouragement just as bad as agreeing to do something I don't want to do? How difficult would it have been to say, "Thanks for inviting me. I'm not the best one to help you promote your new business, but I wish you well with it."

The truth might have hurt—but lying hurts more and betrays the trust between the two of us. Bless my friend's venture, Lord. Help her find just the right person to encourage her. Thank you for giving me the courage to call her this morning and tell her the truth.

## Taking Care of Business

Lord, my husband and I faced facts yesterday. We need to earn more or trim expenses. We started with trimming. We don't need 180 television channels when we only watch about 10. And we don't need to pay for long-distance access on our home phone service when it's included on our cell phone plan without extra charge.

So today I made the dreaded calls to the television and telephone service providers to lower our bills by selecting plans more suited to our needs. I got what I wanted, but it wasn't easy or fast. Customer service representatives are trained to remind people of what they're giving up when they decrease their plans and programs. True, we're giving up something, but it's something we don't want or need.

It takes courage to keep calm and focused during such phone calls. To remain polite, to be clear about what I want, and to continue to say no until the customer service rep has exhausted every option. But I persevered, and I feel good about it! I thanked the women for taking my calls, for informing me of my choices, and for honoring my final selection. They thanked me as well and wished me a good day.

Thank you, dear God, for taking my calls, listening to me explain the plan that I want for my life, and then reminding me why your plan is the best one—and that it's free of charge if I stick to it.

## Packing Light

Lord, the advice we received from the travel company before our summer vacation was short and sweet. "Pack your bag and then the day before you depart, take out one-third of what you packed and leave it home." That's good advice for life too. When I pass by open garages in the retirement community where I live, I'm amazed at the junk people keep—empty boxes, broken bicycles, soiled sofas, car parts, rusty tools, and so on. I want to shout, "Take out one-third, and you'll feel lighter the moment it's hauled away. Repeat this process until you have room to move around and space to park your cars." But I doubt they'd listen to me. People love their stuff, and many keep it right up to the day they die. Then the problem falls on those who are left behind. They have to deal with the clutter.

Try as we might, we can't take anything with us. Our naked bodies will return to dust, and our homes with their trash and treasures will be sold, passed on, or dumped. We go to heaven's gates as free spirits ready for whatever you have in store for us. Now that sounds like very good news to me!

> *We brought nothing into the world, and we can take nothing out of it* (1 Timothy 6:7).

## Peace

Lord, for me, summer is a season to explore your gift of peace—a state of calm and deep, inner knowing that all is well. This is the plane of life I most desire as I grow older. To be serene is to be accepting, to hold life, self, and other people with an open hand instead of a clenched fist because I know my power is limited outside of your grace. One of the most important lessons I've learned (the hard way,

I might add) is to know the difference between what I can change and what I can't. This discipline refreshes my spirit like a stream in a desert when I feel dry and guides me when I feel lost. And for those times when I feel strong and surefooted, your peace enables me to explore new terrain—relationships and places—with the confidence that you are with me every step of the way.

*The LORD God is a sun and shield; the LORD bestows favor and honor; no good thing does he withhold from those whose walk is blameless* (Psalm 84:11).

## Grandparenting Across the Miles

Lord, I love being a grandparent, but it takes more effort when the grandchildren live miles away than it does when they live next door, just down the street, or within an hour or two drive. I don't want the distance to keep me from enjoying them and them from enjoying time with me. As my friend Rita said, "I only get one chance to be a *great* grandma, so I'm going to do it the best way I'm able. I'm building a bond now that will last a lifetime."

I feel the same way. That's why summer is our season to visit the grandchildren in Ohio and to connect with the older ones who are attending camp, going on a mission trip, or working part-time. Handwritten notes, Skype, Facebook, email, and personal visits make a difference.

Help me, dear Lord, to be present to these special people you've put in my life. I want to leave a legacy of love and godly wisdom.

## Happy July Fourth!

July Fourth. Independence Day. Freedom. Liberty. What a gift from you, God! Last year Charles and I appreciated this gift all the more during a visit to Washington, DC. I loved touring the sites, visiting the galleries and museums, and hearing the stories that make up our history as a nation. Lord, you have set me free as an American but, more importantly, as one of your followers. I know the truth that you are the Son of God—and because of what you did for me by your death on the cross, I am free indeed. I don't deserve this gift. I didn't earn it. I didn't even realize what I had until I turned my life, including my will, over to your care. Thank you for leading me to that decision by the power of your Holy Spirit.

## Granddog Tanner

Lord, thank you for Tanner. I love him so much, and I know he loves me. When I show up with my hat on my head, keys and leash in my hand, he's ready to go wherever I lead—but preferably along the route he's familiar with. We enjoy our little "sniff walks." He sniffs and I walk. When he's finished exploring an area, he "heels" and away we go. I love it when he looks up at me as if communicating, "Isn't this fun, Grammy?"

"It sure is, Tanner-boy!" I remark. "It's one of the highlights of my day—just you and me together on a walk. No pressure, no timeline, no one to interrupt us."

As I write about Tanner, I'm reminded of my first dog, Topsy. That little black-and-white pup was the love of my life at one time... until Mom couldn't take his nonsense any longer and sent him to a "big farm with lots of land for him to explore and enjoy." You knew, God, that my heart was broken. How could Mom send our little dog away? I cried into my pillow at night for weeks. I still think of him and feel weepy.

There is something very special about faithful pets that love us without reservation. They seem to be made in your image, Lord. You love and are faithful without question. How blessed I am to have a God and a granddog who love me unconditionally.

## Rocky Island

It's that time of year, Lord, when my heart wrenches a bit—not as much as it used to, but still a little. My adult kids and their families go off to Catalina Island for a week of "fun in the sun," as the saying goes. I can't go along even though I'm grandma to the children and would like to be part of the action.

This is just one more of the crummy results of divorce. My ex-husband lives there now and has vacationed on the island for years. It's a favorite spot for his wife's side of the family, so my kids join them for this one week each summer. It would be pretty weird to be among them—even though part of me wants to.

I'm over the deep hurt of the divorce. After all, it's been more than 30 years now, but in some ways it feels as if it happened last week. A woman I'd seen only at a distance walked into my life, grabbed my husband, and ran off. Of course, it didn't really happen that way, but it sure felt like it at the time.

On the other hand, Lord, you entered my life shortly after that and not only saved my life for all eternity but brought me a new husband who loves you and me with every fiber of his being. And I'm the better for that. How strange that what I saw as devastation led to my salvation.

## Humility

Lord, you say in the Bible, *"Those who exalt themselves will be humbled, and those who humble themselves will be exalted"* (Matthew 23:12). That's what I want to talk to you about today. I need a big dose of humility. Sometimes I'm so filled with my own thoughts, ideas, opinions, and perceptions that I can't see beyond myself. I think I'm humble when, in fact, I'm acting *proud* to be humble.

It's so easy to look at others and judge their behavior and beliefs while forgetting to take the plank out of my own eye, as you remind me in Matthew 7:5. Today help me be a vessel of kindness, love, and other-centeredness. May I be all about humility in the true sense of the word. I want to avoid putting my view of myself above my view of others. Everyone is your child and you gave your life on the cross for each one. No one is more or less precious in your eyes. May I always remember that.

## A Time Apart

"I'm missing you already," my husband said. We were holding hands last night as we sat on the sofa and watched a movie. He seemed close to tears. I heard the shaking in his voice. We'll be apart for a few days while I'm off teaching a journaling class for women. It's wonderful to know I'll be missed, but it feels like both a blessing and a burden right now. My mind dives into that place I try to avoid—feeling like I should stay home. Are we too old to be away from one another? What if he falls or has a stroke? Will I feel responsible because I chose to be away? On the other hand, such a thing could happen even when we're together. I can't take on the world!

God, you're in charge, so I'm going. My bag is packed, and I'll be out the door and in the car this afternoon. I'll hug and kiss my husband really well—and say goodbye *for now*. I know we'll be with each other again soon. Meanwhile, I ask you, dear Lord, to watch over both of us and keep us safe so we'll be sitting on the sofa once again next week, holding hands and watching a movie.

## Seashells

"Over here, Magah!" my granddaughter shouted. "Look at all these pretty ones." I moved down the beach to where Johannah was sitting. Her cup was already half full of beautiful seashells. She spread them out for me to see. "Can I keep them?" she asked.

"Of course!" I replied. "Let's clean them up. Then you'll have some beautiful souvenirs to remind you of our day together."

We washed each one, noticing how the pink and yellow and pearl-colored flecks danced in the sunlight as we rinsed away the grit.

I stood up, brushed the sand from my legs and hands, and took a deep breath. Such a simple activity, Lord, yet such a sweet connection. The years between us disappeared as quickly as our footprints in the sand. I can't imagine anything more wonderful than that moment with Johannah on the beach. She was seven years old then, dear Lord, and now she's almost twenty-four. Thank you, God, for the ability to remember.

## Beautiful Cumberland Falls

Dear God, thank you for Cumberland Falls, so beautifully located in the Daniel Boone National Forest in Kentucky. It was very special to visit my husband's home state this year with his family. I remember reading about one of your natural wonders—a lunar rainbow called a "moonbow"—that occurs at the base of the falls. According to local lore and the brochure, it's the only place this occurs in the western hemisphere! What a gift—nothing mankind creates can compare.

As the Scripture says, if I don't praise you for these splendors, *"even the stones will cry out"* and *"the trees of the field will clap their hands"* (Luke 19:37-40; Isaiah 55:12). As for me, I'm crying out praise to you with them and clapping my hands in thanksgiving.

## A Powerful Thunderstorm

Lord, here I am sitting in my daughter's backyard looking at the fallen branches and twigs brought down from the rainstorm. As I lay in bed last night listening to the clouds clapping, the rain pouring down, and the wind whipping the trees, the noise was so loud I got scared for a moment. Then I remembered that you are more powerful than any natural force because you created it all. In such moments I see how small I am and how much my security and safety depend on your grace and guidance. I'm comforted knowing that when the storms of life blow in unexpectedly, I can turn to you— leaning on you and trusting that these troubles will pass because you love me.

I remember one such storm the day I received a call from my husband that my father was close to death. I was on a camping trip with my women friends at the time—about four hours away by car. The moment we came out of the mountains I changed clothes and drove straight to the nursing home, arriving in the nick of time to say goodbye. Thank you for giving my sister and me special time to tell Daddy we loved him before he took your hand and crossed over to the other side.

After that, a flood of memories rained down on me, and the winds of change blew. I knew life would never be the same again. My father had been a strong and steady presence in my life for 60 years. But I also knew that he was in your hands. Now when I think of my father, I smile and rest in the calm that replaced the storm.

*He who dwells in the shelter of the Most High will abide in the shadow of the Almighty. I will say to the Lord, "My refuge and my fortress, my God, in whom I trust!"* (Psalm 91:1-2 NASB).

## Rainbow Beauty

As I looked out the window of my hotel room in Blarney, Ireland, I saw a most beautiful arc of many colors in the sky. I stared at it for a moment, realizing, dear Lord, that I was seeing you in this rainbow, just as I found your presence in the pastures of grazing sheep, in the castles I toured, in the rolling hillsides, and in the streams and meadows as our coach made its way along the country roads. In that moment I remembered your word to Noah after the great flood:

*This is the sign of the covenant I am making between me and you and every living creature...I have set my rainbow in the clouds...Whenever I bring clouds over the earth and the rainbow appears in the clouds, I will remember my covenant...Never again will the waters become a flood to destroy all life* (Genesis 9:12-17).

I take comfort in those verses again. No matter how far I roam or what condition I'm in, your covenant with me—and with all your people—will never change. It's the same now as when you made it. The rainbow is the perfect visual for me, reminding me that you are with me no matter where I go and no matter what occurs in my life. Thank you for being my God yesterday, today, and forever.

## A Neighbor's Kindness

Lord, what would I do without my neighbors? Thank you for giving me such a caring community of people—on the block, around the corner, and in front and behind our house. Everywhere I look there is a loving person eager to lend a hand when needed. And I feel the same way toward each one of them.

One neighbor holds an annual barbecue and prepares tasty ribs for all to enjoy. Others agree to pick up our mail when necessary or share a daily newspaper. And many are available for a quick chat as I walk around the block, stopping here and there to exchange a few words while they mow their lawns, exercise their dogs, or sit on their porches soaking up the sun.

It's comforting to have good people to share life with, to help carry each other's burdens, and to bring a smile or a word of encouragement when needed. We do that for each other, and for that I'm so thankful.

*Be devoted to one another in love. Honor one another above yourselves* (Romans 12:10).

## Suffering and Loss

O dear God, my friend is facing a huge challenge this summer—physically and emotionally. Everything is up for grabs. Her health is weak, her husband's health is failing, and her family lives far away. I'm sad seeing her situation, and I help as I'm able. But at the same time, I'm excited about the possibility of her finding you through her suffering and loss. I know you are here for her—and for everyone going through similar circumstances.

*[The LORD] was pierced for our transgressions, he was crushed for our iniquities; the punishment that brought us peace was on him, and by his wounds we are healed* (Isaiah 53:5).

I know that at times of suffering some people turn away from you, dear Lord, wondering how you could allow such pain. But we humans are not puppets or robots. That's how you created us! We're subject to the ups and downs of life on earth. Stuff happens. The important point I want to remember and hold up as a shining light is that you carry people through and give life eternal to those who choose to stand with you.

## Squirrels in the Park

Lord, I recall my encounter with squirrels in the yard of our summer cottage in Idyllwild, California. They were everywhere! I loved to feed them peanuts and then watch them eat some and squirrel away the rest. Then last year, while visiting Washington, DC, my hubby and I sat down on a bench in Lafayette Park, across from the White House. We were eager to relax after a long walk and enjoy feasting our eyes on the national treasure in front of us. A fast-moving squirrel caught my attention as he scrambled up a tree, out on a limb, and then scampered down the other side and took refuge in the grass. Maybe to catch his breath? Although I was in the park to get a good view of the president's house, I was thinking of you as I watched the scampering critter.

I realized the little fellow was using the talents you gave him. He could run, dart, crack a nut while holding it in his front paws, stash a supply of food for winter, and entertain those around him as he dashed up a tree, using his keen eyesight and long claws to guide him.

I learned a few lessons from that bushy-tailed fellow. He didn't question himself or hold back from doing what he was put here to do. He just did it! Could the same be said for me? Or am I hesitating to accomplish certain things you want me to? *"Each of you should use whatever gift you have received to serve others, as faithful stewards of God's grace in its various forms"* (1 Peter 4:10).

On another day, I was distracted from eating while I sat by a window in a restaurant observing a determined squirrel poke his claws into a metal mesh bird feeder to help himself to the stash. Even though the feeder was hanging high above the ground on a metal pole, this hungry creature made his way to the side of the container and clung to it for dear life, anchoring his hind paws to the mesh while using his front paws to poke and prod until he released the tasty seeds. He didn't cease his hard work until his belly was full and the supply of seeds was depleted. The birds in the area would be in for a surprise when they came to feed.

Who knew you would use these determined animals to teach me a life lesson as I sat there watching them do what came naturally?

## Bless the Surfers

The kids are out there, Lord, riding the surf, catching waves, falling off their boards, paddling in to shore, grabbing a drink and food, and then going back out again. From the youngest to the oldest—kids, and moms, and dads, and maybe some grandparents too—tall and short, lean and stout, the surf's up for these folks on the weekends in my community, especially during the summer.

Take care of them, Lord. Bring them back safely without nicks and scratches or concussions and broken limbs. It looks pretty scary to me. Swimming? Well, okay, I'll give it a go if I can stay close to shore. But venture out further? No way, except to get baptized—and even then the water was a bit scary to me.

I remember the time I got pulled under when I was 19. I thought for sure I was a goner, but just as quickly as I was towed out I was tossed back. I've never again taken the ocean for granted. It looks friendly but it can be a foe when I least expect it. Thank you for being with the surfers in and out of the water—especially the ones in my family.

## Oh Those Kids!

Lord, last night I watched a movie, and one of the lines struck me hard: "Don't count on your children to keep you warm. Once they grow up they never come back." Ouch! I feel that way sometimes even though I know my children love me, and they'll be here when I really need them.

Meanwhile, I'm taking the advice of a woman older than I am. "I'm doing as much for myself as I can," she said. "I only call on my kids if there's something I can't handle, so when the time comes when I truly need help, I won't feel bad about letting them know."

So far so good at my house. My husband and I are in good health, and we take care of ourselves, our home, and our cars. We still pay our bills without messing up the checking account. We give you all the thanks for helping us keep our ducks in a row and our heads on straight. I miss the days when the kids were little, and we were their whole world. But I also remember the challenge of raising them and how tired I felt at the end of each day. I'm going to learn from all this and go back to living one day at a time, trusting you for the details.

## Pinhead Moments

One friend reached into her purse for her cell phone and pulled out the TV remote. Another put on a pair of earrings, but when she looked in the mirror she realized she was wearing two different kinds. Back to the jewelry box to make the switch—and when she checked again she was wearing the other two! Help, Lord! These pinhead moments are getting the best of my friends, and I'm not above them either. I opened the pantry yesterday looking for a chicken to defrost, and when I finally checked the freezer I noticed a box of crackers in there.

The best we can do is chuckle and keep going, though such events can be alarming. I don't want to spend all my time undoing the mistakes I made while in the *Twilight Zone*. Please, Lord, help me wake up and stay awake until bedtime. Remind me to stop, look, and listen before I make a decision. At this stage of life, time may not be on my side, but *you* are—and you always will be! That's good enough for me and more than I deserve.

## Too Much Talk

Lord, between the phone, the TV, the mall, and the radio, I'm overwhelmed sometimes with talk. I wish everyone would take a "word break," and bless the universe with silence. Am I saying this just because I'm getting old and can't handle all the noise from gizmos, gadgets, and garbage trucks? Maybe so. But whatever the reason, I'm in favor of taking some time in the no-talk zone.

I'm tired of corny jokes, stories I've heard a dozen times, email forwards that are no longer fresh or funny, long phone calls, and salespeople pitching their wares at my front door. And I'm fed up with my own bundle of words. Do I really have anything important to say? Or am I simply exercising my jaw in order to be part of the crowd?

Help me today, dear God, to count my words, and make the words I say count for something that points people to you. And if I can't think of anything worth saying, remind me to lock my lips until I do.

## Mirror! Mirror!

Let's face it together, Lord. I'm getting *old*. And what's worse is that I'm *looking* old. Yes, those are the bare facts. The wrinkles are deeper, the lines below my eyes are rounder, and my eyelids are sagging even more than before. I don't want to succumb to the knife or to some costly cream that probably won't work, but still I find it a challenge to look in the mirror and acknowledge the truth.

It helps to step on the scale because the number that comes up is the same one that was there when I graduated from college. I'm slim by nature, so that's a blessing I'm thankful for. And it's nice when my husband pats my backside and says, "Not bad for an old chick." He makes me *feel* young and attractive again, if only for a moment or two.

On the other hand, getting old has its advantages. I believe I have more wisdom now. I know I have more experience. And I'm positive I'm heading in the right direction—toward heaven where I'll be blessed with a new body that will be forever beautiful and energetic. I feel better already!

## Woody Wagon

Lord, I'm thinking back a few decades to summers in Wauconda when I was a carefree kid. One of my favorite activities was sitting on the back of Uncle Bud's woody station wagon. With legs dangling and arms around each other's shoulders, my cousins and sister and I hung on as the woody bumped and skidded over the dirt and gravel country roads. Those were the days before seat belts and air bags. Less safe but more fun! On other days we'd go for rides in Uncle Bud's freshly painted rowboat. The shiny oars sparkled in the sun as we lowered them into the water and took turns rowing across the lake.

Those were the true golden days. I treasure the memory of them now that the cottages, and roads, and stores, and picnic areas are gone, replaced by modern houses and paved streets. Thank you, God, for such summer days when my whole life lay before me, when everything was shiny and new and unexplored and exciting, when I had no idea what was ahead, and when it was more fun to look forward than backward. I wanted to grow up and make my own choices and try new things. I bless the memories and the wonderful people who helped me make them. May they rest in peace with you.

## Aunt Janet's Potato Salad

Backyard potlucks and summer picnics are as alive in my mind today as they were in the moment years ago. My mother and father loved to entertain family and friends, but our small house couldn't hold a large gathering for long so we spilled outdoors and carried on our feasts at the big wooden table on the grass.

I remember Aunt Janet's potato salad, my mother's apple pie, Dad's grilled hot dogs and burgers, and big juicy watermelons. Of course, we also had plenty of lemonade to go around two or three times. I can still taste its goodness.

Family, friends, and food just naturally go together regardless of the seasons of life. Afterward, it's fun to sink into a comfortable chair and chat with a good friend or favorite relative while sipping iced lemonade or hot coffee.

Lord, you knew the importance of food and fellowship. You provided for your followers on many a hot day in the hills. You multiplied fish and bread so everyone could eat and be satisfied. And you ate with your friends on your last night on earth.

Thank you, dear Lord, for your provision—family, food, friends, finances, fun, and so much more. As I grow older I'm more aware than ever of your bounty and blessing. I've never wanted for anything I truly needed.

## Castles in Ireland

Lord, as I think back on my recent trip to Ireland, I'm reminded of what a special time it was. I can still taste the hearty potato and leek soup, remember the stays in beautiful old hotels—one of them a refurbished castle, recall the clapping and keeping time to the music accompanying Irish dancers and singers, and reminisce about the strolls through the streets of quaint towns and villages with my husband, Charles.

But the highlight was finding you, God, in the castles of Ireland! It took my breath away. As I listened to the tour guides share the history of these magnificent buildings, some of them now in ruins and others in good repair and operating as lodgings, I saw the parallel between the protection these fortresses provided for people of ancient times and the protection you provide. *"Whoever dwells in the shelter of the Most High will rest in the shadow of the Almighty. I will say of the* Lord, *'He is my refuge and my fortress, my God, in whom I trust'"* (Psalm 91:1-2).

I'm also reminded of these lines from Martin Luther's famous hymn "A Mighty Fortress Is Our God" (1529):

> A mighty fortress is our God,
> a bulwark never failing;
> our helper He, amid the flood
> of mortal ills prevailing…

What a relief to know that people no longer need to shield themselves within stone castles or forts. On the other hand, the threats to our moral and spiritual lives are as great today as ever. Only you can be my true fortress. You continue to assure me of your constant care, protection, and guidance. Thank you!

## Prayer for the Restless

Lord, there are so many people wandering the streets, sleeping in doorways, squatting in parks, not knowing what to do with their lives. They're scared, hopeless, and filled with fear—and in many cases probably drugs and alcohol too. Even some who have homes to go to choose to live as though they are among the forgotten and lost. They are restless and downtrodden in spirit, wondering what to do next and who they can turn to for help and consolation. Find them, dear God, and rescue them as you did me in my darkest hour.

# Note This

Lord, I'm happy to realize the value of taking notes—as my mother advised me to do from the first day I could write a sentence. Now more than ever I need these reminders. Keeping a pad of paper and a pencil on the coffee table is an idea whose time has come. That way I can jot down what comes to me and be certain that if I forget something all I have to do is refer to my notepad.

But it backfires once in a while. Just yesterday I went into the kitchen for my morning tea and found a note on the table. Hmmm…I wondered who'd left it. I always place my notes on the coffee table in the living room. Then it all came back—and I must have turned a few shades of red. "Read notes from last night," the note on the table said. That did it. I had come to the point where I had to write an additional note to remind myself to read the original notes I'd written! What good was the reminder if I couldn't remember that I'd written it? God, is there any hope for me? I hope so because it's not likely to get any better! Send a large dose of grace, ASAP. Thank you. Now for a long summer walk to clear my head.

# Bless This Mess

God, it's that time of year again—when the surfers and their gear crowd the beaches, bring sand into our houses and cars, and clear out our pantries and refrigerators. "What's for dinner? I'm starving!" is a popular refrain in my home when the grandkids visit after a day in the ocean.

Their voices are also lilts in my ears because they signal that I'm needed and wanted—especially my cooking. And when they clean their plates and scarf down my apple crisp, I'm in heaven. There'll come a day when I can't do this anymore, and then I'll have only my memories of these precious times. So bless the mess in my kitchen and bathrooms, Lord, and help me focus on what really matters—having family around to love, and hug, and cook for.

## Pots and Pans

Lord, I left the front stove burner on today—long after I'd dished up our morning oatmeal and washed the bowls. What's with me these days? How about the time I put the kettle on to boil, and then saw a neighbor outside and ran over to have a chat? I never gave the kettle another thought—until I returned home and saw the blackened bottom. I can always replace the kettle but not my mind! As someone once said, "I don't mind losing a sweater or a pair of socks. But losing my mind really hurts."

Fortunately, I noticed the lit burner before I left the kitchen this time. Thank you for reminding me. From now on I'll set the timer every time I put a pot or kettle on the stove. Now if I can just remember to stay close until it goes off.

## Fruit Smoothie

On a hot, summer day, nothing is more refreshing than a cold drink. My favorite, Lord, is a fruit smoothie. I like to pull into a shopping mall parking lot, jump out of the car, and walk into a smoothie shop to order a mango–peach blend with an extra boost for my immune system. I enjoy the refreshment and the time to cool off and rest for a bit before I carry on with my day.

And when I do, Lord, I can't help but think of you and the fruit smoothie you create in my spirit: *"love, joy, peace, forbearance, kindness, goodness, faithfulness, gentleness and self-control"* (Galatians

5:22-23). Yes, the fruit of the Holy Spirit is the best kind! It's the one that lasts and is never empty.

Thank you for showing me the parallel between the natural and the supernatural. Nothing is wasted.

## Mountain High

Lord, thank you for a week hiking in the Mammoth Lakes area with some of my women friends. I enjoyed the blessing of feeling your presence the day we rode the gondola to the top of Mammoth Mountain and then hiked down the five miles to the valley floor.

The views you created are spectacular. Everywhere I looked and walked I was reminded of your power of creation. I remembered the beautiful verse in Isaiah 55:12:

> *You will go out in joy*
> *and be led forth in peace;*
> *the mountains and hills*
> *will burst into song before you,*
> *and all the trees of the field*
> *will clap their hands.*

I clapped my hands right then with the trees. And every day I went forth in peace, and my spirit burst into song.

## Rock of Ages

God, thank you for the blessed opportunity to stand in the cleft of the great rock in Burrington Combe Gorge in North Somerset, England, where hymnwriter Augustus Toplady found shelter in a storm. He later wrote the inspiring hymn "Rock of Ages" (1776). It was one thing to read the history of this man and this place and quite another to experience it for myself. I will never forget it. Thank you for using Toplady to write a song of praise that would so power-fully communicate the gospel and encourage the saints to the degree that his name and story are still being shared to this day. Lord, I pray his words to you today.

*Rock of Ages, cleft for me,*
*Let me hide myself in Thee;*
*Let the water and the blood,*
*From Thy wounded side which flowed,*
*Be of sin the double cure;*
*Save from wrath and make me pure.*

## Little Mouse

Lord, remember the July morning I reached for my breakfast food in the back of my station wagon at the campground? My plastic bag holding nuts and dried fruits was badly punctured. When I picked it up, most of the contents fell out. *Oh no! A field mouse maybe?* It was time for our group's morning hike, so I decided to deal with the matter later. Big mistake, right Lord?

To my surprise, when I returned several more bags were full of holes. Even my tissues were perforated. Flies and mosquitoes were all around, so I chalked it up to life in the outdoors.

At the end of the week, my friends and I broke camp and said our goodbyes. The next morning, after a good night's rest in a motel, a terrible stench hit my nose when I opened my car. *What is that?* Suddenly I noticed a small, dead, furry creature curled up in a little open box I'd left on the floor behind the driver's seat. A long tail hung over the edge. A field mouse!

"Eek!" I shrieked and shivered at the sight. The poor fella must have snuck in when my car door was open and then died in the extreme heat of the day after I locked up.

I called for help, and one of the employees at the motel came to my rescue. "A dead mouse!" I told him. "I can't bear to touch it. Will you please remove it for me?"

The man chuckled, reached in, and carried the little guy off, box and all.

I thanked him and we went our separate ways. But then I had a shame attack. It was just a field mouse, after all. Why did I make such a big deal out of it, God? He was one of your dear creatures. And if you could make a place for him on the earth, surely I could allow him to help himself to a few nuts and berries.

Lesson learned. Thank you, Lord. I've never looked at field mice in quite the same way again.

> *Ask the animals, and they will teach you,*
> *or the birds in the sky, and they will tell you;*
> *or speak to the earth, and it will teach you,*
> *or let the fish in the sea inform you.*
> *Which of all these does not know*
> *that the hand of the LORD has done this?*
> *In his hand is the life of every creature*
> *and the breath of all mankind* (Job 12:7-10).

# Autumn

*On the tenth day of the seventh month you must deny*
*yourselves and not do any work...*
*because on this day atonement will be made for you,*
*to cleanse you. Then, before the LORD,*
*you will be clean from all your sins.*

LEVITICUS 16:29-30

*"Every leaf speaks bliss to me, fluttering*
*from the autumn tree."*

Emily Brontë

# Schooldays

Dear Lord, it's that time of year again, time when the grandkids go off to school—some to elementary, some to high school, and some to college. I love participating in their autumn rituals. Shopping for clothes and school supplies is part of the fun of getting them ready for a fresh start.

I've created one of my own traditions with them too. My contribution is a back-to-school lunch and pedicures for my two granddaughters and their mother who live near me. I enjoy seeing our pretty feet as we leave the nail shop to enjoy a hearty salad or soup at our favorite bakery and cafe. The following week it's off to school for the kids, each to take up the tasks in front of them—listening, learning, and applying lessons to their lives.

Every autumn I return to school as well, even though I'm a college graduate of many decades. I sign up for a class at church, dig in to the Bible, and read the book our pastor has written for a new study. I welcome the reminders and promises that you are with me no matter what stage of life I'm in. Lord, your lessons are precious to me, especially now as I grow older.

*So then, brothers and sisters, stand firm and hold fast to the teachings we passed on to you, whether by word of mouth or by letter. May our Lord Jesus Christ himself and God our Father, who loved us and by his grace gave us eternal encouragement and good hope, encourage your hearts and strengthen you in every good deed and word* (2 Thessalonians 2:15-17).

## Falling Leaves

God, thank you for the memory of driving through the Morton Arboretum in Lisle, Illinois with Mom and Dad one autumn day years ago. I can still picture my father at the wheel, my mother in the front passenger seat, and me in back—all of us taking in the beauty of the autumn splendor together. Decades later, after I was married, my husband and I visited Kentucky Lake near Paducah, Kentucky, with my in-laws to view the glory of autumn in that part of the country.

Our parents are gone now, just as the leaves on the trees have fallen, making room for the new growth in spring. As I age, my colors are changing. And on my appointed day I'll fall too, returning to the earth in body while my spirit soars to the heavenly place you have prepared for me. And so the cycle of life continues. Thank you for allowing me to be part of it and to contribute to it, dear Lord.

## Autumn Decor

My husband blessed me today, God, by decorating the dining room table with festive autumn leaves, pumpkins, gourds, and ornamental ears of corn. I'm getting excited about this new season as we close out summer and look forward to the holidays that provide plenty of reasons to celebrate and share. I'm already thinking about making crockpot applesauce, lentils with sautéed onions, and baked chicken.

I plan to feed my soul, as well. I'll read a new book, attend a concert, spend time in the Bible, and nurture my spirit with lots of long walks in the woods and along the beach. I also plan to be more receptive to the words you have for me as I call out for guidance. This autumn I want to fall into your arms to learn and rest because the cold winds of winter are just around the bend.

# Trick or Treat!

Halloween is almost here, Lord, and the grands are excited about choosing a costume or creating their own. Even their mom and dad dress up. It's fun to watch the parade of kids in their neighborhood march down the street and go up to the houses with their bags open for candy. No one comes to our community of seniors. I guess they figure we all go to bed early.

This holiday always brings back memories of my sister and I walking up and down our street in Boulevard Manor and my dad standing on the curb to keep an eye on us. When our trick-or-treat time was up, we'd dash home, plop on the living room floor, and tear into our bags, picking out a few pieces to eat before Mom had us put the stash away for another day. Those times so long ago were good. I miss the carefree state I was in then—the simple joys that made up my days and the close-knit feeling of friends and family around me.

Many decades have passed since my last trick-or-treat night, and decades have gone down since my children walked our neighborhood. Before long the last of my grandchildren will have passed through that phase of their lives too. God, how did my children grow up so fast, and how did I get this old so soon?

# Grandma's Cookies—Not

O Lord, here I go again. I know the grandkids would love it if I donned a flowery apron and came bearing a plate of cookies made from scratch. My daughter would probably love it too. But I sure wouldn't. Baking isn't for me, pure and simple. I like to *write*. Maybe they'll appreciate that about me after I've gone to heaven. Yes, I've baked cookies and made some yummy cakes in my time, but it's always a stretch. I don't want to eat sweets myself because I like feeling fit and looking as good as I can for being a grandma.

Sugar doesn't help me achieve those goals. I'll play a game, draw a picture, take a walk, even climb part way up a tree with my grandkids, but please don't ask me to *bake* for them.

Every autumn this refrain replays in my mind. The old shoulds descend upon me like bears to honey. I try to whip up some enthusiasm for the task. Wouldn't it be nice to bring a platter of Butter Horns or Chocolate Delights or Sweet Macaroons to my daughter's home? The answer is, "Yes, it would." But I still don't want to take the time to do it. I'm not pleased with my attitude, but there you have it. I hate to bake. I'll write a story to share with them instead. Okay?

## Carrot Soup

I like homemade carrot soup; my husband does not. What should I do, Lord, make soup for one? With all the petitions your people bring before you, this seems like a trivial one. And yet what I love about you and depend on is your willingness to hear from me on any subject. In fact, you are so far ahead of the game that you often answer my concerns before I even utter them.

I remember when I wanted to find a knitting class. One day I inquired at a knit shop in my area, and there seated by the door was a knitting instructor! I joined her class and attended for two years.

When my computer printer retired from active service, you sent me to the exact aisle in the office equipment store where one that would meet my needs had just been placed on sale. When I worried that I wouldn't be able to install it, you gave me an "atta girl" for encouragement. I followed the instructions, and the machine hummed to life, saving me a $79.95 technician fee. How cool is that?

Thank you for hearing, and answering, and delivering solutions.

Now, Lord, back to the carrot soup. I hear you. Make it for myself, resulting in fewer carrots to prepare, less cash outlay, and a smaller pot to wash. Got it!

## Cast On, Bind Off

Lord, I ordered the book *Cast On, Bind Off* from Amazon.com. It arrived this week, and I'm eager to get into it to find ways I can "cast on" and "bind off" knitting stitches to give my garments a first-class look. While thinking about this activity, I'm reminded of what you say in your Word: *"Cast your cares on the LORD and he will sustain you"* (Psalm 55:22). Unfortunately, I don't follow this mandate often enough.

When I do cast my cares on you, the next thing I know I've taken them back and fallen into the trap of trying to sort them using my own strength. Soon I'm mired down. Help me, please. Life is so much sweeter when I cast my cares on you.

*"Whatever you bind on earth will be bound in heaven"* (Matthew 18:18). You said this to your apostle Peter when you made him the head of the church, giving him authority to direct Christians in their faith. I'm thinking I should apply this to myself as well. When I make a promise, I want to follow your lead and bind myself to it. Surely then I will lead a first-class life.

## A New Normal

Fourteen years ago this month Charles and I received some scary news. He had prostate cancer. My husband was only 70 years old at the time—old to someone in his thirties, maybe, but not to us. We'd hoped to live a long life together, walking, talking, laughing, praying, and traveling side by side. What could this diagnosis mean? Because of my husband's age, the doctor recommended against radical treatment. He'd found a minimal amount of cancer in just one of six samples, so he took an optimistic view. "You could easily live a long and normal life," he said. "Let's wait a while and see what happens."

We made a follow-up appointment for three months later and walked out of the office, one trembling hand in the trembling hand of the other. We prayed and watched and waited over the coming months—and we've been doing so for the last decade and a half. Thanks to you, Lord, there has been no increase in the cancer in any direction. This disease may very well outlive my husband. We are so grateful.

The cancer has impacted our intimacy, but we've settled into a new normal with lower expectations and higher levels of gratitude for being alive and together. Physical intimacy is a special part of marriage, for sure, but being available to one another in other ways can be special too. We now enjoy each moment of our days and nights, taking life as it comes instead of making unreasonable demands on each other or on you, dear God, our creator and redeemer. Thank you for good health when we have it, for comfort when we don't, and for your presence through it all.

## Mother's Apple Slices

Lord, what is autumn without the fragrance of apples baking in a pie or in a delicious cobbler? The only thing that tops those treats are my mother's apple slices baked in a flaky crust and drizzled with a powdered sugar-based frosting. I can still smell and almost taste her signature dessert. I never make it myself. I'm not a baker, if you'll recall. However, I do like to remember what Mom's dessert was like, drawing from all the years I lived at home and the yearly visits after I left home to marry and start my own family.

Sometimes a memory is almost better than the real thing—especially now as I diligently watch what I consume in my older years. What's important to me about Mom's dessert now is the love that went in to the task. I can picture her rolling out the dough, placing it carefully in the oblong pan with floury hands, packing the crust and container with apples sprinkled with cinnamon and sugar, and then closing up the package with more dough. Then she slit the top dough with a knife here and there to allow the steam to escape while cooking.

When she removed the pan from the oven and drizzled the frosting over the top, my mouth watered. A generous helping of love and apple slices, along with a glass of cold milk or a cup of hot tea, were all I needed to feel content.

Today, as an older woman myself, I return to that memory time and again. I take comfort in it. Mom wasn't quick to share her love through touch, but she did so with the bounty she served from her kitchen. That's what I most remember and treasure. Thank you, God, for my mother and for the love you gave me through her.

## Field Hands

Lord, as I drive by the farm fields that surround our community, I'm drawn to pray for the dear ones bent over as they plant, pick, and pack the crops. Harvest time knows no holiday. While I enjoy a festive holiday meal with my family, the young and old labor in the orchards and vineyards as though it's just another day. When I go to the market at the corner or push my cart up and down the aisles of the grocery store, loading up on the food we need for the week, I think of the sheer drudgery that went into bringing the produce to this destination. How blessed I am.

Take care of your sons and daughters in the fields, dear God, and bless the work of their hands. They are your servants to be sure, and now I realize they serve me too.

## Sunrise, Sunset

Lord, sometimes I feel as though my days have lost their middles. The sun streams into our bedroom window early in the morning, and it seems that before I turn around twice the sun is setting. Autumn days shorten. Daylight is slim, and the cool air of evening replaces the warm sunshine of the day. What did I accomplish? What have I left undone? What can I do to retrieve what feels like lost hours? But then I remember your words: *"Commit to the Lord whatever you do, and he will establish your plans"* (Proverbs 16:3).

As long as I start my day with prayer and conversation with you, all will be well. My life isn't measured by how many goals I reach, but whether or not I walk with you in whatever I set out to do. Thank you, Lord, for leading the way. I think I'll sit down now and enjoy a cup of tea—with thee.

## Bring on the Garlic!

Autumn days remind me of Girl Scouts, and county fairs, and Sunday matinees at the local movie theater. I especially enjoy going to the fair, Lord. I love seeing the pig races, the flower show, and the watercolor art display. Then there are the lovely quilts, knitted goods, antique furniture. And I can't forget my favorite activity— eating garlic fries. I only eat them once a year, but I never miss. People don't want to get near me after that, so I save the treat for the end of the day just before going home.

My husband loves garlic too, so we indulge together. He once told me that if there was such a thing as garlic ice cream he'd stand in line for it. I'm not willing to go that far. A few years ago he was challenged to make good on his promise. We attended the Garlic Fair in a town near our home, and sure enough a vendor was selling garlic ice cream. My husband backed off, deciding that garlic fries were enough for one day. "Maybe next year," he said.

I won't hold him to it.

## Nothing like Down

The night air creeps through my open window. Time to close up the house and crank up the fireplace to take off the chill. And time to pull out the down comforter. It feels so cozy when I slip beneath it at the end of a long day. My weary bones respond to the feel of the soft warmth, Lord, just as my spirit takes comfort when I feel your presence surrounding me. I take a deep breath and let it out slowly, methodically, and then take another. The day's cares disappear into the darkness.

You remind me in the Bible not to worry about tomorrow because *"tomorrow will worry about itself. Each day has enough trouble of its own"* (Matthew 6:34). For sure.

But each day has many beautiful experiences too, especially when I leave the driving to you, Lord! I look forward to waking up with my husband at my side, the sounds of birds announcing the dawn, and then the sun streaming through the sliding glass door of our bedroom. I don't know what is ahead, but I can be sure it is good—even when something *seems* bad—because you are good. It's sure nice to take another few minutes to snuggle under my down comforter.

## A New Watch

My husband showed me the new watch he purchased at a great savings at our local department store. The silver face and black leather band looked very attractive on his wrist. And best of all, the battery was guaranteed for five years. A month later the watch went kaput. So much for promises and guarantees. He took it back to the store for repair, and wonder of wonders, the clerk exchanged it on the spot for a brand-new watch. How nice!

This event reminded me of your promises, Lord. They are good for life—not just for 5 or 10 years. When we come to you with our broken lives, you exchange them for new life in you! We don't have to produce a sales slip or beg for what we want. You are already ahead of us, waiting for us, ready for us, and always willing to cover us with your grace.

> *If anyone is in Christ, the new creation has come: The old has gone, the new is here!* (2 Corinthians 5:17).

## Your Story Matters

I received a small notebook as a gift. It even came with a little pen. I keep it at my desk. The cover says "Your Story Matters." The idea is to jot down notes, and words, and thoughts, and sayings as they occur. They don't have to have any rhyme or reason to them. They don't have to amount to anything more than a collection of miscellaneous musings. I don't have to write a book or a blog with the information. I'm free to scratch out whatever I wish and then read and keep, read and discard, or read and whatever else catches my fancy.

Since I live in a world of deadlines as a professional writer, it's nice to have a spot where I can meander with words and see where they lead without having to create something for publication. It feels like a holiday from work when I write for only me. I wonder what I'll come up with once I open it and let my mind discharge what is in my holding tank. I'm excited! I might even learn something new about myself. Wouldn't that be neat?

## Silence

Lord, have you noticed I'm talking less and listening more? I'm beginning to like the gift of silence. I never expected to, and I never really wanted to. Yet here I am looking forward to the quiet, to the space to think and dream and pray and ponder. Autumn seems like a good time for this, although any day is appropriate. But as the year comes to an end, I find myself gearing down, taking it easy, reviewing what I've done.

*"Yes, my soul, find rest in God; my hope comes from him"* (Psalm 62:5). Unless I stop, I can't rest. And if I don't rest, I can't hear. And if I don't hear, I won't listen. So here's to a new season of stopping, resting, hearing, and listening to you in the silence, dear God. May I always hear what you say to me.

## The Wind at My Back

Lord, the wind was fierce today. I felt as though I were being whisked around the block instead of just walking around it. I can't say I enjoyed the shove because I didn't! But I took a lesson from its boldness. Sometimes I need a good push in the right direction or I'm apt to take the easy way. I'm happy you keep after me, reminding me of the ultimate prize worth working toward: *"I press on toward the goal to win the prize for which God has called me heavenward in Christ Jesus"* (Philippians 3:14).

Thank you, God, for giving me opportunities each day to love someone, to meet a need, to share a word of encouragement, to take a step of faith, and to close my eyes at night with a prayer of gratitude on my lips.

## Prayer for My Sister

God, my sister asked me to pray a special prayer for her, and so I do so here. Please bless her in her illness. Heal her if it is your will. Whatever you do, give her acceptance and peace in you. Take the fear and worry and anxiety, dear Lord, so she can experience your rest and comfort and make decisions based on your counsel, trusting that you will guide her to the right path. Let her know you're with her as she travels the road you have her on.

## What Do I Know?

"What do I know?" This was the question a woman asked today as a group of us sat in a circle of support, listening to each other's challenges and giving one another our attention rather than our advice. What a blessing that is...and so rare in the fix-it culture of today. The woman seemed bewildered as she hid her face in her hands and quickly pushed away any encouragement offered by another. She may not know all the facts involved in her search for answers to her dilemma, but she has access to your Holy Spirit, who knows and reveals all things as needed. I pray for her and the others I know who feel so small in your presence, God. May they grow in their understanding of themselves, of others, and, most of all, of you. You are our loving Creator and Lord, so we can ask for and receive exactly what we need.

# Talented Fingers

"Fingers can paint, point (this can be good or bad), do needlework, tie a shoe, hold a pen, write, type, play a musical instrument, shoot marbles, pick up a shell, scratch a back, tickle a foot, soothe a baby, massage sore muscles, plant a seed, pick a flower, caress a face…the list is endless," wrote my friend Margaret.

I agree, although I hadn't thought much about these talented digits before reading her reflection. Not only can our fingers do many things—and sometimes many things at once—but no two people have the same fingers…or fingerprints. What a blessing, Lord.

"Innumerable environmental factors influence the formation of fingerprints," states Dr. Michael Roizon, who explained that the process starts in the womb. "The exact position of the fetus at a particular moment and the exact composition and density of surrounding amniotic fluid that's swirling around the fingers as they touch surrounding structures determines the unique 'print.'" Psalm 139:13 says, *"You [LORD] created my inmost being; you knit me together in my mother's womb."*

Margaret finished her reflection with a goal for the day: "To express more gratitude and not take for granted the gift of even the small things—like our fingers." When we pay attention to our unique fingers, Lord, we're inspired to use them for your glory in all things.

## Chocolate Paradise

Charles and I have finished dinner. It's time for our treat of the day—a single square of sumptuous Ghirardelli dark chocolate. My husband likes his with mint crème in the middle. I take mine straight! I don't need two squares—just one. I bite off a small piece and savor the bittersweet blend as I relax after a full day and a full meal. All is well, dear God, and chocolate has its place in my sense of well-being.

It doesn't take much to satisfy my urge for something delectable. I'm off of pies and cakes and ice cream. I don't need the calories or the fat. And none of them do the trick anyway.

Your promises, as well as your commands, dear Lord, often strike me the same way chocolate does. Raw, sometimes harsh truth combined with words that are as pleasing as honey. They remind me that life has a measure of bitterness and sweetness. In fact, both are necessary to achieve balance.

*Blessed is the one whom God corrects; so do not despise the discipline of the Almighty. For he wounds, but he also binds up; he injures, but his hands also heal* (Job 5:17-18).

## A Dollar and a Dream

Lord, I saw this sign on a billboard once: "It only takes a dollar and a dream." For many men and women, that's all they need to lead them to the nearest casino or gambling website, especially during the days of autumn when cool weather and staying indoors can lead to loneliness and longing. Thousands of older people begin a slow descent into compulsive gambling. Some, however, find you when they wake up to the destruction they're causing themselves and their loved ones. But others never recover.

I pray for people caught in the gambling web today. I know a man who has spent most of his adult life taking chances and risking everything, and now he's penniless. Women too fall into the trap as they look for something exciting to do with their time after they retire or if they've lost their spouses. God, please turn their hearts and minds to you. Speak into their lives before they run through their savings, inheritances, and Social Security checks. Lydia is such a woman. She continued gambling until she squandered $200,000. I pray for her and others who are victims of this often-hidden illness. May they find their joy in you and engage with others in healthy ways that will bring them the happiness they're looking for.

## Trash or Treasure?

Lord, I think of you as I drive or walk through my community on Saturday mornings and see all the "Yard Sale" signs in yards, garages, and fields. From used clothing to kitchen gadgets, your provision is evident. I love seeing the friendly smiles and overhearing the neighborly chitchat as buyers enjoy a glass of lemonade or a cup of coffee while fingering various items and then checking their wallets for the money needed to make a purchase. I like the spirit of friendliness and generosity I see. Sellers earn a few dollars, and buyers take home items they want or need. As the saying goes, one person's trash is another person's treasure.

> *Feed the hungry, and help those in trouble. Then your light will shine out from the darkness, and the darkness around you will be as bright as noon* (Isaiah 58:10 NLT).

## Holiday Moments

Dear Lord, it's that time of year when the holidays tumble in one after another. First Halloween, then Thanksgiving, Christmas, and New Year. So much fun to look forward to, especially with our grandkids. But lots of work too. There's shopping, cooking, wrapping gifts or writing gift checks, signing cards or creating a holiday newsletter, and hosting brunches and dinners. I love it all, but I can't do any of it without your grace and guidance. So I pray for those today and for the presence of your Holy Spirit as I jump into the fray and still hope to retain my peace of mind.

## To Do or Not to Do

Dear God, as I flip my kitchen calendar to a new month, I'm reminded of the many things still undone from last month—emails never written, articles still in outline form, flowers that need tending, and drawers and cabinets crying for an organizing hand. Should I transfer these leftover tasks to the clean, unspoiled page before me? Or should I drop them and start fresh? Time. If only there were more of it, or more energy to accomplish my goals in the time I do have.

Our culture is inundated with time-management tools—datebooks, pocket calendars, wristwatches with built-in alarms, beepers, smart phones, books, computer programs, and seminars on how to save, spend, invest, maximize, and catch time before it flies away.

God, what I really need to do is find your perspective on productivity. What if time were not so much the fleeting, tyrannizing resource we're taught to believe it is? What if, instead, I choose to view time as an expression of you? As part of your very nature? Would I then be so eager to live by deadlines, join the morning rat race, or grab a minute and run with it?

Time spent with family, with a sick friend, with a homeless person, with a man or woman celebrating a special occasion is truly an expression of your love. Those moments may be more productive than completing a career goal. When I practice your perspective on productivity, I find there is plenty of time for work and play, ministry and rest as I weave the threads of my allotted time into a tapestry of eternal significance.

> *Do not forget this one thing, dear friends: With the Lord a day is like a thousand years, and a thousand years are like a day* (2 Peter 3:8).

## For Our Military Men and Women

Lord, I watched former Arkansas governor Mike Huckabee on his TV show *Huckabee* the night he interviewed the father of a brain-injured soldier. The soldier's life will never be the same again because of what he suffered in battle. It was so difficult to imagine the impact of this condition on the young man and his family. Yet finding your presence in the lives of this soldier and other military men and women isn't hard when I see the strength of their faith and the support of their families. The father of the soldier said his faith alone carries him through each day.

Dear God, please bless and protect the thousands of soldiers who've been afflicted in one way or another in the line of duty and who return home. Most have to make significant adjustments, and some are unable to put their lives back together in meaningful ways. Some soldiers need care for the rest of their lives. We owe them so much gratitude, love, and loyalty. Be with them day and night, dear God.

## Ah, Fashion!

Lord, I wonder if you care about fashion. Certainly there were no dress codes in your day on earth—or were there? From the accounts in Scripture, it seems tunics and sandals were "in" for attire. Recently I read in a newspaper that shoulder pads, a fad from the 1980s, are definitely out now. (I'd better get rid of those old jackets!) Soft fabrics and slimmer lines are the rage. Men's swimsuits are back to the boxer style "with drawstrings and dignity," as the headline proclaimed. T-shirts and flip-flops are still okay. As I read, I wondered if anyone considered your opinion regarding fashion. The very thought might cause people to chuckle or smirk.

As I see it, the subject is worth considering. After all, you reminded us not to ask, "What shall we wear?" You know what we need, and if we seek first your kingdom and righteousness, you will provide it (Matthew 6:31-33).

I want to look attractive, but obsessing about the latest trends creates stress and competition that takes my heart away from you and the provision you have for me. The next time I walk into a clothing store, Lord, please remind me to think about what really matters—dressing for you, my Lord and Creator.

## A Blessing from You

A friend wrote to me today and asked how she could pray for me. What a blessing! My name came to her mind, and she contacted me. I feel so loved and cared for, Lord. How special to hear from someone far away who wants to lift up my needs to you on my behalf. Thank you for providing me with this dear friend. We're sisters in Christ, and though we seldom see one another in person, we're connected through your Holy Spirit. My day is lighter and more productive now! I feel empowered to do what you've called me to do today.

# A Pressure-Cooker Day

God, today feels like a pressure cooker—and I'm in the pot! I have deadlines to meet, emails to answer, meals to prepare, and a book to write. Help me calm down, live one moment at a time, and entrust the outcome to you.

I was telling someone just the other day how amazed I am that even when I can't imagine how I'll ever accomplish my goals, somehow I do by *your* grace. At the end of the day I go to bed relaxed and happy that I did what I could and trusted you to take care of the rest. As Max Lucado says in his book *Grace: More Than We Deserve, Greater Than We Imagine,* "Grace is God's best idea. Rather than tell us to change, [God] creates the change." Amen to that! I've seen you do this over and over in my life, and I thank you for it.

# Quack! Quack!

One of my favorite children's stories is the classic *Make Way for Ducklings* by award-winning author Robert McCloskey. It was published when I was just three years old. As you can imagine, the book didn't mean nearly as much to me then as it does now. As the story goes, the parents of eight ducklings needed a bit of help finding a safe place to raise their brood. During a rest stop in Boston's Public Garden, Mr. and Mrs. Mallard agree they've found the perfect spot. But when Mrs. Mallard and her darlings are stuck on a busy street downtown, their policeman friend, Michael, rushes in, stops traffic, and makes a way for them.

As an older person, God, I sometimes feel like Mrs. Mallard. I feel stuck in the busy traffic of life. I need a hand—someone to make a way for me so I won't be overlooked or run over. I remember a time when a young man stopped his car to let me cross in front of him. He called out, "We have to look after our older folks." *Older folk? Who's he talking to?* I wondered. *Can't he see that I'm as fit as a farmer?* There's something about the phrase "older folks" that clangs in my ear. I'm not ready to listen to it in reference to me. But maybe I should, since chronologically I am one—an older folk, that is.

That evening the young driver was my "Policeman Michael," making a way for this duckling to cross the highway safely. Thank you, God, for providing such thoughtful people willing to serve. May I be one for another duckling, younger or older, someday.

## A Few of My Favorite Things

Eating oatmeal and peaches with yogurt and maple syrup. Doing the dishes. Reading a devotional and newspaper. Making the bed. Getting dressed. These are my favorite things about today because whatever I do and wherever I look I am seeing you, God. You are all around me. You've given me the food to eat, the words to read, the bed to sleep in, and the clothes to wear. How grateful I am!

> *"Who can hide in secret places so that I cannot see them?"*
> *declares the* Lord. *"Do not I fill heaven and earth?" declares*
> *the* Lord (Jeremiah 23:24).

## Thanks, Bill!

Bill sent me a letter telling me he enjoys my humor books for seniors, including *Gettin' Old Ain't for Wimps*. He said he hadn't laughed so hard in years. What a nice thing to hear! Bill and I have never met, but after he read some of my funny stories he felt he knew me. After I read his letter, the feeling was mutual. I've sent him a couple books as a thank-you for becoming a fan. He made my day.

Thanks, dear God, for bringing people into my life I can inter-act with and enjoy. It's so easy to make new friends when I focus on sharing laughter and joy instead of peddling my complaints. I'm not typically a negative person, but I have my moments. I'm reminded of the verse in your Word that says, *"Clap your hands, all you nations; shout to God with cries of joy"* (Psalm 47:1). Bless Bill, dear Lord, and all who call on you.

## Mango Lemonade

I'm treating myself to a cold glass of mango lemonade—a sum-mer delight—even though it's autumn right now. Our community along the Pacific Ocean is catching up with the rest of the hemi-sphere after a cold-start summer. I wore my Ugg boots almost every day of July and August! How crazy is that? My flip-flops sat in my closet waiting for the weather to behave itself.

You keep us guessing, Lord. I'm never sure what to expect, but that's probably good. I heard once that when my expectations are high, my serenity plummets; when my expectations are low, my serenity soars. Makes sense when I think about it, which is some-thing I should do more often. Instead, I get myself into trouble by planning too far ahead and wishing I knew what was coming next.

Life is easier, happier, and more serene when I leave everything in your hands and simply live for your glory one day at a time.

## Numbers

Lord, it's that time of year when my husband and I want to get things in order—money, clothes, pantry, garage, and garden. We're settling in for the coming winter when we'll hunker down and stay indoors more. The days will be shorter and the nights longer. The spreadsheet is laid out on the desk, and pencils and pens are poised for use. Charles likes to keep tabs on paper rather than using the computer. Doesn't matter to me as long as the numbers are recorded and we make sense of them together.

Where do we need to cut? What can we afford? Are there clothes to give away? Can we justify a splurge on a new sweater or pair of pants? And how many cans and boxes are sitting in the pantry waiting for us to open and use? The garden is looking pretty good now that we weeded, trimmed, and planted some new flowering shrubs. The ice rose is blooming, and the princess plants are boasting their large purple blooms. I love being among them. They provide such beauty and comfort. They take my mind off the numbers and help me put things in perspective again.

Thank you, Lord, for flowers, and money, and clothing, and food. May I always keep in mind that all of it comes from you, and I will never be without as long as I look to you for guidance and wisdom.

## Beach Baptism

Lord, my baptism at the beach weeks ago was one of the most profound events of my life. I'd been baptized as an infant, and my husband was baptized as a young boy due to his mother's prompting. You know this, of course, but those occasions weren't the same as this one because we are plenty old enough now to understand the decisions we make.

Charles and I wanted to display our faith in the sight of others as a public sign of our trust in you, Lord. It was also to thank you for your grace over the past 30 years that we've been following you. The water was icy cold, but I hardly noticed because I was so excited! As I went under, I buried my old life of sin. As I came up, I rejoiced in being cleansed and resurrected into a renewed life in you, my God. It was quite an experience, and one I won't forget. I love reflecting on what I learned about baptism in the Bible: *"Peter said to them, 'Change your hearts and lives and be baptized, each one of you, in the name of Jesus Christ for the forgiveness of your sins. And you will receive the gift of the Holy Spirit'"* (Acts 2:38 NCV).

Our pastor sent us off with these beautiful verses from the book of Proverbs: *"Trust in the LORD with all your heart and lean not on your own understanding; in all your ways submit to him, and he will make your paths straight"* (3:5-6).

## Quarrels

God, I hate it when my husband and I get upset with one another. I only see my side of things, and, of course, he sees his side. Trying to speak across the fence between us seems to only keep us further apart. I want peace again—the easy harmony that usually characterizes our marriage. But it's difficult to retrieve unless someone breaks the ice with an apology—a sincere one that has heft and conviction, not just a conciliatory phrase for the sake of coming together.

In my recovery group there is a saying: "Let it begin with me." Okay, I will. Even if I believe I'm in the right. I am sorry we're in conflict. Does it really matter who is right and who is wrong about the details? The important thing is that we reconcile and then pray together for a renewal of your grace between us. I'll do that right now, God. Be with me, please, as I make amends.

## Counting Pennies

I remember years ago, dear God, when my husband and I had so little money that we started a penny jar. One night we needed gas for our car and didn't have enough bills in our pockets to fill the tank. Then we thought of our coin collection. We spent the evening counting pennies and came up with enough to pay for a few gallons of fuel. As I think of this incident today, I'm reminded how faithful you are in the big things and in the little things. You even turn a simple task such as counting pennies into a major blessing during a time of need. Thank you for that. When I pull into a service station to fill up, I glance backward in time and realize you've taken care of us through the years in all ways—and you always will.

## Tender Lights

Lord, today's reading in *God Calling* is timely for me. It talks about how you ask your people to count everything lost so we might gain you. "Dreary as that path must look to those who view it only from afar, it has tender lights and restful shades that no other walk in life can give." What a beautiful statement. I am very familiar with the "tender lights and restful shades." In fact, today I am living in that light and resting in that shade. I am at home alone this weekend while my husband is away. I will miss him after a little while, but most of the time I'll enjoy being quiet, looking to you for encouragement and fellowship, and enjoying the time and space to write to you. How special it is to *be*. I want to carve out such times more often.

# Invaders

How amazing are the animals you've created, dear God. I learned about many of them during the weeks I was writing a children's book about invasive species—animals that move in to other animals' habitats and take over. While digging into the subject, I thought about how my habits, attitudes, and viewpoints are often like these invaders. I barge into people's lives and drop my "sins," stealing their peace of mind or robbing them of the thoughts and ideas that nourish them. Perhaps I discount another person's opinion or try to force my way of thinking on someone who isn't open to what I have to say. Or maybe my expressed thoughts are poisonous to them even though I put a smile on my face.

Other people sometimes behave toward me in the same way. They invade my territory, worming their way into my thinking, stealing my joy, upsetting my day. Human beings in such situations leave just as much damage in their wake as invasive species such as the zebra mussel, or the brown tree snake, or the European wild boar do in water and on land.

I'm reminded of your teaching, O Lord, regarding our relationships with others—whether with people or animals, for you made us all. It is up to me to find a way to contribute to peace on earth. *"All of you be harmonious, sympathetic, brotherly, kindhearted, and humble in spirit"* (1 Peter 3:8 NASB).

# Giant Redwoods

Lord, how relaxing it was to enjoy a stroll with my friend through the Redwood Grove in Henry Cowell State Park. The majesty of this place made me think of what heaven might be like—an exquisite paradise filled with hundreds of giant trees, beautiful greenery, and quiet paths where a person can think and pray and bask in the surroundings without worry or care. Oh, how wonderful that will be!

My friend and I were amazed to learn that the oldest trees in the park are between 1400 to 1800 years old. We couldn't help but look up in awe at these giants and the resilience they display. Some have been burned, twisted, maimed by wind and fire, but they stand proud and tall nonetheless. And new trees are growing alongside the old-timers. I was inspired by their ability to bounce back from stress again and again and still go on living after hundreds of years. This reminds me of a specific verse in the Bible: *"The Lord your God is the one who goes with you to fight for you against your enemies to give you victory"* (Deuteronomy 20:4).

If you, dear God, take care of a grove of trees, I can trust that you will take care of me in my old age because I know you love me. I will continue to stand tall, to look to you for direction and guidance, and to trust you in all ways.

As we concluded our walk, my friend and I agreed with the poet Joyce Kilmer who said that only you, God, can make a tree.

## The Potter's Wheel

Cambria, California, is one of my favorite respites. I especially love to walk through the gift boutiques and art galleries. I enjoy the beautiful pottery in various sizes, shapes, and colors that grace the shelves. These collections remind me of your people, dear Lord. We come in all sizes, shapes, and colors, according to your hand. As I watched a potter do his work at a wheel, I recalled words written by the prophet Jeremiah:

> [The Lord said,] *"Go down to the potter's house, and there I will give you my message."* So I went down to the potter's house, and I saw him working at the wheel. But the pot he

*was shaping from the clay was marred in his hands; so the pot-
ter formed it into another pot, shaping it as seemed best to him.*

*Then the word of the LORD came to me. He said, "Can I not
do with you, Israel, as this potter does?" declares the LORD.
"Like clay in the hand of the potter, so are you in my hand,
Israel"* (Jeremiah 18:2-6).

Lord, as I grow older, I see that I can use a good deal of reshap-
ing and resizing. I'm thankful I don't have to take on that project
alone. You can put this mound of clay back on your potter's wheel
and rework it with your hands until it turns out exactly the way you
wanted it to look so I can better serve you and others.

## Washing Cars

Over the weekend my husband and I washed our cars by hand.
We uncoiled the garden hose, pulled out the car-washing soap, and
piled clean towels and rags on a nearby bench. Then we set to work.
However, I have to say this is not my favorite thing to do, especially
as I grow older. I can't reach as far. I'm not as flexible as I used to be.
I'm not as eager to take care of all the little details, such as polishing
the chrome wheels.

"I'd much rather write a book than wash a car," I grumbled as I
worked on the windows. "This is hard work." I wiped my brow and
took sips of water to keep from keeling over in the hot sun.

Then, as I worked, I discovered your presence with me, dear
Lord. And what a difference that made! As the grime lifted under
the pressure of the water and sponge, the beauty of the silver-gray
color broke through and I smiled at the sight. Is that how you feel,
Lord, when you give me a good cleansing through your Word and in
answer to my prayers? You stand me up and hose me down, releasing

me from my mistakes, sins, and goof-ups so I am presentable in your sight once again.

*Cleanse me with hyssop, and I will be clean; wash me, and I will be whiter than snow* (Psalm 51:7).

## A Crown Jewel

Lord, thank you for the gift of being able to visit the forest and the sea on the same day. One visit to Point Lobos State Reserve near Carmel, California, and I see why it's referred to as "the crown jewel of the California State Park System." The cry of the sea lions, the breathtaking vistas, intriguing rock formations, ancient trees, and well-trod trails made it worth the long drive. I loved finding you in every nook and cranny of the place. Your hand of creation was everywhere I looked. When I'm out in nature, I'm as close to you as I can possibly imagine. No church or cathedral can compare. And now that I'm older, such a place means even more to me than it did when I was young. I have no interest in amusement parks anymore... or restaurants or theaters. Take me out for a picnic on a bench or a hearty walk in the woods and I'm happy. Thank you for preparing such a visual feast, dear God.

## Poison Ivy

Lord, as I hiked with friends this week, I noticed large clumps of beautiful red leaves on scrawny twigs on either side of the trail. Some of them were so full and lush they had spread to the trunk of a tree and were climbing to the top. I took a couple of photos and wanted to reach out and touch these lovely autumn leaves—that is until someone ahead of me shouted, "Watch out for the poison ivy. You don't want to mess with it, believe me."

I stepped back and paid closer attention to where I was walking. This beguiling plant, so attractive and, at the same time, so harmful, reminded me of the presence of temptations in our lives. They call out to us with their good looks and intriguing promises for pleasure and happiness, but the moment we give in—whether to gossip, sinful thoughts, alcohol or prescription drug abuse, gambling, or adultery, they spew their poison. Then we have to work hard to recover from their damage, regardless of our ages.

It makes more sense to stay away from such poison to start with. But when we're feeling lonely, or hurt, or depressed, or bored, it's easy to leave the trail you set out for us and take a chance on what appears to be harmless. Thank you for sharing your wisdom on this topic:

> *We have a great high priest, Jesus the Son of God, who has gone into heaven, let us hold on to the faith we have. For our high priest is able to understand our weaknesses. When he lived on earth, he was tempted in every way that we are, but he did not sin* (Hebrews 4:14-15 NCV).

> *[Jesus] can help those who are tempted, because he himself suffered and was tempted* (Hebrews 2:18 NCV).

Thinking of these truths was the best part of the hike. It brought me to my senses and alerted me to turn to you when I'm tempted to stray from your trail.

## Race Walking

Lord, thanks for putting Charlene in my path this week. I enjoyed speaking with her and hearing about her race walking career. She's been all over the world competing in marathons. I'm impressed. At age 80 she's not walking competitively anymore, but she is still walking. She's only a few years older than I am, but I'm holding her as an example for me. I hope that when I reach her age I'll be filled with the same vitality, stamina, and good grace.

Every day I'm grateful to you for my legs. They've served me well over all these years, and they don't seem ready to retire anytime soon. It's such a privilege as I age to be able to walk, and drive, and hike, and swim, and dance. May I do it all for your glory.

## Protection

Lord, I'm thinking of all the men at "Man Camp" this weekend—husbands and dads, grandfathers and single men—who are gathering together to learn more about you and enjoy fellowship with each other. Take care of them, dear God. Look after my husband and give him stamina, a good sleep each night, and wisdom each day as he listens to the presentations, reads your Word, and walks the campus. He was so looking forward to time alone with you as well as time with the other men. Bring them all back safe and sound and wiser than they were when they left. We need strong, committed men in our world, men who love and follow you and set an example for their families and the people around them.

# Shouldering On

Today I'm thinking of one of my grandsons, Lord, and the fun we had hiking and climbing rocks and scouting caves on our trips with the Sierra Club when he was a little boy. Now he's a grown man. Where have the years gone? He's tall and handsome and has a good-looking mustache and beard. He can give the best bear hugs I've ever had!

I remember when he and I hiked to the top of a large hill, huffing and puffing by the time we reached our destination. When I told him I might not always be able to do such a strenuous activity with him, he smiled and said without hesitation, "No problem. When you're too old, I'll throw you over my shoulder and carry you to the top."

Well, God, I'm almost there. Too old to take to the heights, but I'm glad I can still hike the lower trails and gaze at the pinnacles, knowing I was once able to climb to the top of Mount Whitney. This is a good reminder to do what I can with what I have...while I have it.

# Never Too Old to Serve

Lord, I pray for my friend in Fiji. She's an older gal like me, and she signed up to do missionary work there. It's hot and buggy and the accommodations aren't anything like the comfort of her home. Give her an extra measure of strength wherever she is today. Let her know you're right there helping to carry her load. I pray against anything that would stand in the way of her health and joy, and that the men and women she encounters will come to know you the same way she does.

## Time to Vote

O Lord, it's that time of year when the phone rings off the hook with announcements and messages from representatives of political parties. Each one wants my vote, which is understandable. But I'm not sure what to think. One candidate says one thing, and another says something else. They're so convincing, so how do I choose?

Friends campaign through conversation and discussion, wanting me to see their side of things. They want me to get involved, and excited, and motivated to elect certain individuals. I feel pushed around. I don't know what to do. I need time to clear my head and gather my thoughts. I also need to read and listen more, especially when I talk with you. You already know who our next leaders will be. I trust that whoever they are will be for the best, even if I find the results worrisome or disappointing.

Only you, God, know what's best for our country at any given time. I feel relaxed now, certain you will guide my mind, my heart, and my hand when I cast my votes.

## Birthday Blues

How funny, Lord. My friend Eric called his friend John to wish him a happy autumn birthday. Eric went on to say that he liked knowing John shared the same birthday with one of Eric's family members. The common date made it easier to remember. He could buy two cards at once and make two phone calls on the same day.

As John hesitated, Eric suddenly remembered something important. He was the family member who shared John's birthday! Oops! A "senior moment" had gotten Eric again. But he took it well. Eric invited John to meet him for lunch where they'd celebrate together with slices of chocolate cake. Oh my, dear God, we do the funniest things as we get older. I'm choosing to smile about it.

# Checking the Checkbook

Lord, I was in a panic yesterday when I couldn't reconcile my checkbook. I finally found the mistake. At least it was a good one this time—the bank said I had more than I said. I finally discovered I had entered a large debit twice. Silly me! Thankfully my husband and I resolved it, and we indeed have enough money to cover all our bills with some left over to start out the new month.

"We're in good shape. The bank and I agree at last!" I proclaimed. Then I sat back and realized that you're in this chore with me, my Father in heaven. You guided my eyes to the right place. You also help me see where our income goes and even where to cut back when things get a bit tight. You encourage me with wisdom from your Word: *"My God will meet all your needs according to the riches of his glory in Christ Jesus"* (Philippians 4:19). How blessed I am to have you—even when it comes to my checkbook.

# Invisible Gifts of the Heart

Lord, thank you for showing me how I can give gifts to others in small ways and big, depending on the situation. Not the kind of gift that comes wrapped in colorful paper with a pretty bow, but the kind that is usually felt rather than seen. A smile is one way to bless someone. And how about making eye contact? I don't always take the time to do that, but when I do I sense what a gift it is to the other person and to me. Sometimes my silence is a blessing, especially when the other person needs to talk, or cry, or laugh, or share. Just being there without a word may be the perfect gift.

One of the most difficult presents to bestow is a sincere apology. Now that's a gift in short supply in our culture. How wonderful it would be to let go and simply say, "I apologize for hurting you. Please forgive me." I want to give that present more often. Help me,

God, to set aside my pride and admit when I'm wrong. I want to always be ready to give invisible gifts of the heart.

## Sad News

Lord, I received sad news twice today. One friend's father has been diagnosed with cancer; another friend's husband died of cancer yesterday. Life is so uncertain. One minute we're fine, and the next brings a life-changing verdict. But through it all we have you by our side. I know these women do. They'll grieve, of course, but as my friend Wendy told me years ago, "After the sadness, my grief turned to gratitude for the life my husband and I had together. He wasn't mine to begin with. He's always belonged to God." May I remember this courageous statement if I am faced with similar circumstances someday.

## Goose Bumps!

Sometimes, God, I see my life as one long to-do list that will end when I get to the last item. I enjoy crossing off various chores, from dusting to weeding, from baking a casserole to meeting a writing deadline. "Look what I accomplished today!" I shout to my husband as we close the office for the night and look forward to a nice dinner by the fire. Then I realize that even though you're proud of me for doing what you've called me to do, my life is worth a whole lot more than the tasks on my list. Life isn't about *works*. It's about walking with you, watching you, listening to you, and enjoying your friendship. Imagine! I am a friend of God, and God is a friend of mine! I get gooseflesh just thinking about it. I love you, Lord! And I know you love me.

## An Ordinary Day

Today was a day like many others. I got up early, dressed, ate breakfast, tidied up the house, checked phone messages, responded to emails, and did some writing. All in all, it was a very good day.

I feel peaceful.

I feel satisfied.

I feel happy.

Thank you, Lord, for the extraordinary in the ordinary, for helping me find contentment in the small, everyday things that keep my household humming and my relationships in good shape. Most of all, thank you for your love and care. Without it, none of the rest would be possible.

## The Promise of New Life

It was a day in October when my sisters, brother, and I said goodbye to our mother for the last time. Lord, it was a hard day. Memories came rushing back as I took a final look at her in the narrow, cardboard box before the mortician slid the container into the cremation vault. I knew her spirit had gone before her. The mom I knew and loved was already in a better place. I think of her often at this time of year. It's a season of farewells as the leaves fall and the flowers fade. But there is the promise of new life ahead. I hang on to that and trust you for what is next. You never disappoint me.

## How Can I Forget?

Lord, you know my dad enjoyed telling the story of the time he purchased a book on how to enhance his memory. He got off to a slow start! He paid for the book but walked out of the store without it. That meant a return trip hours later when he remembered that he forgot! This yarn is good for a laugh and may even be a bit consoling to those of us who can relate to it. But I prefer to focus on the fact that you, Lord, forget too. You put all my sins as far from you as the east is from the west (Psalm 103:12). You forget about them when I come to you in sincere apology and repentance. How blessed I am to have a relationship with such a God!

## Inspired by the Harvest

Lord, I was so inspired last week listening to the men from Teen Challenge sing your praises at the Harvest Brunch at a nearby church. Those young people, once living out on the street or in prison, are now safe in your arms, healing from their wounds and addictions and living with one another as brothers in Christ. What a powerful experience to watch the blend of ages, backgrounds, ethnicities, and levels of education in this gathering. How sweet to see you bring in the harvest of souls who were once lost but now are found.

# Giving Thanks

We have a ceramic pumpkin on our porch with the words "GIVE THANKS" emblazoned across the front. I like looking at it each day when I go out or come in. It doesn't matter whether it's spring, summer, autumn, or winter because giving thanks is appropriate all year long. I especially like to focus on giving thanks as we approach Thanksgiving Day. It's time to put on the dining room table our pilgrim figurines, dried autumn leaves, and a basket full of gourds, including squash and mini pumpkins. Cinnamon-scented candles complete the scene.

But, Lord, the most important thing is my heightened sense of appreciation during this holiday time. Sure, a turkey dinner with all the trimmings is nice to anticipate, especially pumpkin pie topped with real whipped cream! But without an attitude of gratitude to go with all this, what's the point? It would be just another meal eaten and forgotten by the next day. As I grow older, what matters now more than ever is the time I take to survey my life and the amazing blessings you've sent my way from my childhood right through these senior years. They're too numerous to count and even to recall them all.

When I take a moment to dwell on a time past, another gift from your generous hands pops into my mind. Memories of little things really delight me, like sitting in the crook of a tree whittling a piece of wood with my new Girl Scout knife, ice skating on the frozen pond in my hometown, and comparing bowling scores with my grandfather who outdid me every time.

Yep, Thanksgiving dinners and family gatherings have always been special, but they become more precious as I age because the table gets larger every year as the number of children, grandchildren, and someday even great-grandchildren expands. But most of all, I love the quiet hours after the meal is eaten and the dishes are done. That's my time for reflecting on what it means to be truly thankful. You have blessed me "real good," and I thank you for it.

## A New Middle Name

My husband has given himself an additional middle name: "Grateful." Whenever people ask his name, he includes this new one. And when they ask how he's doing, he answers, "I'm grateful." Charles appreciates his life, my life, our family, our home, our church friends, our freedom, and most of all his relationship with you, O Lord. It brings me joy to see the gratitude on his face and to hear it expressed in his conversations. Oh that all of your people would sing your praises and hold up their hands in gestures of thanksgiving! You have given us so much. May we always remember to say thank you and mean it, considering all the things we have to be grateful for—freedom, shelter, food, clothing, jobs, family, friends, and so much more.

But most of all, we need to give thanks for your protection, abundant provision, care, and love. Even those who don't know you in a personal way know in their hearts there is a power greater than themselves. I pray for them right now and ask you, Lord God, to speak to them this year about the wonderful plan you have for their lives and the joy of spending eternity with you.

## Bare Bones

Our Japanese maple tree is now bare, preparing for winter, it seems. I'm sad when I look out the window and realize all the beautiful red leaves are gone until springtime. But that's the way of things, isn't it, Lord? Birth and death with life in-between. Autumn is a poignant time for me—a reminder of the passing of minutes, and days, and weeks, and months, and years. My husband and I have been in this house for six years now. Our grandchildren were little when we moved in, and now two are teens and one is a preteen. I'm so glad we got here when we did, even if it seems like the deal came through in the nick of time.

The seasons of nature and the seasons of my life are coming and going at a rapid pace. One day I will be down to bare bones myself—until you whisk me to heaven and clothe me with a new, glorified body. I will shout, "Hallelujah!" to you on that day when time as I know it will be no more. Your presence with me and mine with you will be my joy.

## Settling Down

I'm making strides at going paperless, dear God. I even have the Bible on my iPhone now! I also look up verses on my computer when I'm working at my desk. For me, at least, there is no substitute for holding the bound version, but sometimes it's nice to catch a verse on the run. It also feels good to unclutter my office of all the little bits and pieces of paper that slow me down because of loss or misplacement. Where's that phone receipt? The invoice for a bill that was due last week? The slip of paper where I'm sure I jotted down an email address? Yes, little by little I'm making progress.

I can apply this practice to my spiritual life too. So often I make things difficult by purchasing too many books that end up in piles or promising friends that I will meet for coffee and prayer when I know I'm already overcommitted. I need to settle down and put things into the proper perspective—your perspective. You don't expect me to be perfect, but you do encourage me to rest in you. When I do, I can find what I need, discard what I don't need or want, and have enough time to be with the people who matter to me.

## Memory Shenanigans

Lord, it's one of those days again. You know the kind. I walk into the bathroom intent on brushing my hair, but then I notice the hand soap container is almost empty, so I carry it to the kitchen to refill. I return to the bathroom, trying to remember what was on my mind when I left. Then I see my hairbrush on the countertop. I must have already used it, so I put it back where it belongs—in the top drawer.

I notice the drinking cup has a few drops of water in it. That must mean I already brushed my teeth and rinsed my mouth. Good. Teeth and hair are taken care of. I'm making progress. On the other hand, maybe I didn't brush my teeth. Maybe I simply took a drink of water. How can I be sure? If the toothbrush is wet then yes, but if it's dry then no. Maybe I brushed with my electric toothbrush, and that's why the manual one is dry. I give up. I take a swig of mouthwash and let it be.

What's the deal here, God? There's not much hope for me if I can't even remember the simple routines of my day. But such shenanigans do bring a chuckle. That alone perks me up! I decide to brush my hair and my teeth for the first…or second…time, happy that I still can. Thank you for that.

## GPS Angel

Off we went, dear God, tooling down the highway. My friend was at the wheel, her husband was in the passenger seat, and my husband and I were seated in the backseat. Charles was relieved to see a map light up on the dashboard—the vehicle had a built-in GPS system. That little "angel" would see to it that we reached our destination in good time and by the best route.

Later, Charles and I decided we were in awe of this amazing tool.

If we had one in our car, there'd be no more struggling with paper maps, no more disagreeing with one another about where to turn, no more stressing while trying to read street signs in the dark, and no more doubting our ability to get from here to there without an accident or long delay. Once more we have reason to praise and thank you, God, for the gift of advancing technology. The next stop for us is the car dealership to have our very own GPS angel installed!

I'm even more thankful, Lord, that we won't need one to get to heaven. You lead us there through your Son, Jesus Christ.

## Out to Lunch

Lord, please give me the ability to hang on to my mind even if my body eventually fails me. I feel so sad when I see people oblivious to what's going on around them. Sometimes it can be funny, as it was when my friend set a bottle of water on top of her car while juggling her purse and keys and then drove off unaware that the container toppled into the street. Yep, for that moment she was "out to lunch," as the kids say.

Other times memory lapse is no joke, especially when people are "out to lunch" because of mental decline due to advancing age or infirmity. My prayer today is that you will comfort and console them when that happens. Please help all of us stay close to you in thought, word, and action. I never want to be out to lunch when you're speaking to me.

## Our Good Neighbor

Thank you, O Lord, for the good neighbor who found my husband's wallet in the movie theater after we left. He took it home and left us a phone message right away so we could retrieve it in record time. If only life were that simple all the time! When we mess up, overlook a detail, or create a distraction, how nice it would be if honest, helpful neighbors were there to help us make things right again. I was so touched by that man's kindness. I want to be just like him when an opportunity to be a good neighbor comes up for me.

And sure enough, you delivered one! I met a woman on a camping trip who needed someone to talk with. She was boiling over with anxiety and worry over a problem in her life. As I listened, she relaxed and then thanked me for helping her solve her problem. And all I did, Lord, was smile and listen. How easy it was to be a good neighbor and friend. May I never forget that lesson.

## Covering My Tracks

Lord, I'm amazed at how quick I am to fib, to fudge, to just plain lie when I'm embarrassed, humiliated, or simply don't know what to say. You're so right in your Word. *Pride* is usually the culprit, and it does go before a fall. That trait has caught me trying to cover my tracks more than once. I don't like to admit I forgot to visit my friend when I said I would, I neglected to bring a dessert to the autumn potluck, or I overlooked sending my daughter a birthday card. The truth is, I don't like to appear foolish in people's eyes. Help me overcome this flaw, God, and to become the person you created me to be. I want to be transparent even when I've made a mistake.

# File Mania

Lord, the other day I received a frantic text from a friend I'd been shopping with. "Did you notice what I did with the receipt for the sweater I bought at Macy's this morning? I can't find it anywhere!"

I admitted I hadn't paid attention. I assumed she'd tucked it into the shopping bag. But no, it wasn't there…and it wasn't on the dining room table or the kitchen counter…it wasn't in her pocket, purse, or car. It had disappeared. We finally agreed the store could issue a replacement.

Minutes later my friend phoned me. "Receipt found right where it should be—in my Macy's folder in the file cabinet. I'm just too organized for my own good!"

We both laughed, grateful that, as always, God had come through. He always does—sometimes right away and sometimes when we're about to tear our hair out over our harebrained escapades. Thank you for affirming that senior moments can provide opportunities for us to turn to you instead of relying on ourselves and, thus, falling even deeper into a hole filled with confusion and fury.

# The Secret Cake

God, a chill is in the air. It's time for fall cleaning, making soup, and enjoying Auntie's secret cake. I've never tried baking the cake, but I enjoyed the taste of it when I was younger. I'm not sure I have what it takes to create her masterpiece—patience, time, energy. But when I think of my auntie, I remember the hours she spent in the kitchen making wonderful cakes and desserts that smelled so inviting and tasted even better. But her secret cake was the best. Fragrant vanilla or chocolate layers with lemon pudding between, and then frosted with butter cream. It sent my taste buds singing when I was a kid. *Yum!* That's the perfect word to describe this delicacy. Her secret? Vanilla or chocolate wafers were gently and precisely inserted beneath the bottom layer to heighten the finished appearance and prop up any areas that didn't rise properly. I'm chuckling just thinking about it. I don't know how many people knew Auntie's secret. I just know that I felt special when she confessed it to me. I miss my auntie with her sweet smile, lilting voice, and secret cake.

Why do we seem to appreciate people more after they die? Or remember with deep fondness the things they were known for? I don't have an answer, but I know for me it's often so true. Suddenly lightning strikes, and nothing is the same ever again. Lord, that's all the more reason to live in the moment and to relish it! This time will never pass this way again, and neither will the people we've loved and cherished and lost. Help me to be here now and give my best to each moment, to each person, to myself, and, most of all, to you. This is one secret I want to share with everyone I meet!

## Just Visiting

Lord, I hope I never have to live in a nursing home. I'd rather be a visitor like I was last week when I spent time with my brother-in-law who is suffering from dementia. I experienced so many emotions as I walked around the facility and noticed many people sitting in wheelchairs, unable to move from place to place without assistance. The caregivers were patient and kind and did all they could to meet the needs of their residents, but still I felt a sadness I couldn't deny. I hoped all these dear people would soon be called to heaven so they wouldn't have to endure another day of living in bodies that were breaking down and minds that could no longer hold a thought. I don't mind visiting, Lord, but I don't want to live there.

When I got home, I realized that I'm a visitor even in my own home. I don't belong to this realm. I am, like all the people who love you and follow you, here for a brief time. Whether from a nursing home or our own homes, we're only here until you call us to our real home in heaven with you.

# Winter

*As long as the earth endures…summer and winter,*
*day and night will never cease.*

<small>GENESIS</small> 8:22

⚬⚬

*"Winter is the time for comfort, for good food and*
*warmth, for the touch of a friendly hand and for a talk*
*beside the fire: it is the time for home."*

Edith Sitwell

# Only Five Minutes More

"Five more minutes," my husband pleaded as he slipped his arm around my waist and pulled me into a spooning position. It was seven o'clock on a cold winter's morning—time to get out of bed and put on the oatmeal. It was still chilly in the house and dark outside. I gave in to the warmth of his embrace. It felt good to me too, reminiscent of an old song from the 1940s titled "Five Minutes More."

I'll probably repeat that phrase over and over during the day. I need just five minutes more to finish the article I'm writing, or to answer an urgent email, or to return my daughter's phone call, or to get dinner on the table. Lord, time is slipping away so fast it makes my head spin. But then I remember that time is in your hands, and you're not in a hurry. So why am I?

You call me to a comfy chair to sit a while with you and listen, to be still and know that you are God. When I respond to you, my day is so much sweeter. And by the time I lay my head on my pillow at night, I heave a satisfied sigh because I had plenty of time to do all that you asked of me that day. All I need then is five minutes of prayer before giving in to the peace of sweet sleep.

# Getting Old Is...Getting Old

Lord, this aging business isn't much fun sometimes. And I feel it more in winter because I'm sensitive to the cold. Right about now it's time to crank up the furnace and pull out my granny sweater to ward off the chill. I haven't always been this way...but then I haven't always been this old either! My skin is a bit thinner these days, and my bones feel the wind. Photos of me from just a year ago leave me wondering who that woman is. Have I really aged this much and so soon?

Pictures of my husband and me at Disneyworld 20 years ago when I still had dark brown hair, which is now snowy white, surprise me. And don't get me started on how fast that change occurred! But thank you, God, for promising that even to my old age and gray hairs (white too, I hope) you will sustain me because you made me (Isaiah 46:4).

## Hard Times

My friend called this morning with sad news, Lord—but it wasn't news to you because you are already there, comforting and caring for her as she comes to grips with her mother's death. I wanted to be a good listener, but I kept thinking back to the day my sister called with the news that our mother had passed away minutes before. I broke out crying on the spot. It wasn't a shock. I knew it was coming. But the certainty and finality of her passing left me limp.

When I let myself relive those dreaded feelings as I hurried to my friend's side, the memory helped me be fully present for her. Instead of relying on clichés like "Well at least your mom lived a long life— 95 is a feat in itself" or "You know she went straight to heaven," I reached for my friend's hand and held it while she cried. I wish someone had done that for me.

## None of My Business

Lord, two of my friends are in a fuss with one another. It hurts my heart to watch and hear about it. I love them both. I see each side of the argument. I want to stand between them, placing my hands on their chests and begging them to 'fess up to their wrongs and make amends. But it's none of my business. I have fences of my own to mend. Remember when you told me to row my own boat and trust you to instruct others on how to row theirs? It's not as easy as it looks. I have so many good ideas—so much wisdom—if they'd only ask for it! Are you smiling, Lord? Such an ego I have. Good thing you keep bringing me down to size with your tender reminders to lean on your understanding instead of my own.

## Pasta's On!

I'm making a nice, hot dish for dinner on this cold night. My husband has flipped the switch to our fireplace—yep, no real logs and no ashes for us—and I'm heating a large pot of water for pasta.

"How do you want your sauce, honey?" I call over the blaring news on the television.

"Plain and no meat!" he shouts above the clamor.

But I don't take him at his word. I decide the man does not get enough vegetables in his diet, so I toss into the pan of tomato sauce a little onion, a few mushrooms, and some spinach clippings. A few minutes later we're sitting side-by-side on the sofa, taking in the news, and eating this cozy meal. Charles doesn't say a thing. He just cleans his plate and thanks me for a delicious dinner. *I got away with it, Lord!* I think. I smuggled some greens into my darling, and he didn't even notice. Or did he?

As I take his plate from his hand he winks. "You're a clever one," he says.

I'll take that as a compliment.

## Santa Face

It's time to pull down the Christmas boxes, haul the fake tree into the living room, line the windows with colorful lights, and decorate the tree. Can you tell I'm not excited about what's ahead? Lord, it seems like a lot of work to me. At this stage of life, I'd be satisfied with the tabletop tree we put in the kitchen window. The tiny ornaments and winking lights are just right. I can put together the whole ensemble and pack it up after Christmas in 10 minutes.

But it's not enough for my husband. He's a "Christmas freak," which is how he refers to himself. He loves draping garland around the china cabinet, placing berries and colored balls in flower vases, and hanging our stockings with care from the knobs on our entertainment center.

Most of all he enjoys placing the little Santa-face lightbulb front and center on the tree—just below the small wooden crèche. The bulb doesn't light up anymore, but it did a long time ago when Charles was a boy in his parents' home. It's the last remnant he has of those Christmases past.

When we move on from our earthly home, he hopes one of our kids will pick up the little Santa and carry on the tradition. I'm not sure that will happen. They have families of their own now and are creating customs they hope their children will remember. And so it goes—one generation after another celebrating Christmas in its own way. But most important, Lord, is the tie that binds all of us together—your birth. We may deck our halls with boughs of holly, but we proclaim in song and story your coming, the one tradition we will never minimize.

# The Big C

Twice this month I received word that a good friend has been diagnosed with breast cancer. It sounds like a prison sentence, like a warning of a winter storm brewing. My heart aches for them. I had a mammogram a few months ago and received a clear report. Thank you, God, for that news, and please be with my friends as they pray for your guidance about their treatment.

I remember when my sister and my best friend went through their process in dealing with cancer. Both are longtime survivors now—one more than 20 years and one more than 10. You carried them through. I learned from watching on the sidelines that we can get past anything if we follow you. This is good to remember whenever I receive difficult news—the loss of a job, or the death of a parent, or the collapse of finances. When winter hits, we know that spring cannot be far behind.

# Knit One, Purl Two

I seem to pick up my knitting needles more often when the days grow short and the sun goes down. "Blah, blah, blah," drones the TV news anchor as I knit one, purl two during the evening news report. The small basket beside my chair is filled with colorful yarn—a skein for a scarf, a ball for baby washcloths, and a bundle for a blanket. I'm not sure I'll get to all of these projects, but I can dream, can't I?

I used to type until midnight sometimes when the writing bug hit me. I can't do that anymore. I can't knit into the late-night hours either. I'm gettin' old, God. I need more rest. A nap sounds good a couple of times a week, and slipping into bed by nine o'clock at night feels delicious. Then I have time to speak with you in prayer and read a snippet or two from the Bible and a few pages from a novel before dozing off. But if I take it easy, slow down, do what

I can and not push myself too hard, I'll get my books written and those scarves and washcloths completed! It just might take all winter, but that's okay. I'm not in a rush these days.

## Every Moment

Lord, on this chilly, winter day, I'm taking warmth from the words on a plaque that a friend gave me for my birthday this year. The author is unknown but I sure like what he or she wrote:

> In the happy moments, praise God.
> In the difficult moments, seek God.
> In the quiet moments, worship God.
> In the painful moments, trust God.
> In every moment, thank God.

I'd like to practice all these disciplines all the time, but I know I'll forget so the framed presentation is a good reminder. As I grow older, there is an abundance of happy moments if I pay attention and don't allow myself to dwell on the difficult or painful ones. I also want to enjoy the quiet moments after so many years of noise—raising rambunctious children, boisterous neighbors who partied till the wee hours, and blaring horns and sirens in city traffic.

When it comes to the bottom line, seeking you in all ways and in all things with worship and trust and gratitude is the only way to have the happy moments that turn my heart to praising you.

## AB&J

Lord, peanut butter and jelly is a favorite lunch or snack in our house all winter long—like fresh strawberries are in summer. My husband loves this PB&J combo, and the grandkids do too. When out of ideas, I can always pull down the familiar jars and a loaf of their favorite bread.

I, however, prefer AB&J—almond butter and jam. And apricot is my first choice in jam. There is something hearty and satisfying about a slice of bread toasted to a golden brown and then smothered in these delights. Top them off with a cup of mint tea, and I'm set for the afternoon. Have I ever stopped to thank you for this treat? Probably not, so I'll do it now. Thank you for AB&J...and PB&J too. Little things like these make days sweeter.

## Ah! The Desert

It's one of those weeks in winter that seems *so* long, Lord—like it will never end. I ache for a break and time all by myself. I want to grab my tent and camp stove and head for the desert, where it's warm and dry and there's plenty of space to spread out and just be. I don't want anyone to go with me. I want to be alone. I'm tired of noisy conversations, phone calls with endless chitchat, and people knocking on my front door trying to sell me this or that. I'm even fed up listening to me! *Quiet* is what I want. And simplicity. A granola bar and tea for breakfast, an apple and a wedge of cheese for lunch, and a bowl of thick, hot soup for dinner. Then off to bed in my sleeping bag under the stars (unless it's raining).

But I probably won't take this trip except in my imagination. I'm too old now to be trooping around the desert without a companion. What if a coyote shows up? Or a tarantula crawls into my tent? Or I plant my face in a cactus if I trip while hiking? No, my desert foray isn't going to happen, Lord. But I know you understand my desire because you often withdrew to the desert for time to pray and think and commune with your heavenly Father. You *get* it—that deep need to flee the mundane, to let your spirit soar, to leave the everyday behind—at least for a little while.

I feel better just talking about it and knowing you're with me in this. You got fed up too because even though you were divine, while on earth you were human as well.

I realize there's nothing to stop me from going to the desert in my imagination. Yes, I'll do that for sure. See you there!

## Dancing in the Dark

Lord, sometimes I think courtship was more fun than marriage. When we were dating, Charles dined and danced me. I felt pretty, wanted, sensual and loved. I still feel loved, but we don't dance anymore. We talk about it, but we don't do it. And we're good dancers. We cleared the floor when we were on our last cruise! And, of course, we do a couple rounds at a wedding if the music is right for us. One New Year's Eve we danced at home in front of the fireplace in our Ugg boots. Not terribly romantic, but we held each other close and that felt good.

Will there be dancing in heaven? I hope so because I won't have any tasks to hold me back, or fatigue to get in the way, or old age to cramp my style. Yes, there are times I want to toss all inhibitions to the wind and just dance with my husband, not just with my grandkids to the beat of their Wii program. However, if that's all that's available right now, I'll take it. My husband can sit and watch if he wants to. But if you ask me, he's missing out.

# Restore My Joy

Lord, sometimes it's a challenge to hang on to my joy. I receive a call from a relative or friend with disappointing news. He or she can't make our Christmas party after all—and I don't find out until I'm about to put on the buffet and fill the punchbowl. Or on my way to the department store an impatient driver cuts me off and misses my car by a hair. I have to pull over to catch my breath.

Or I hear about a fire that swept through an elementary school, killing three young students.

Snails invade our flower garden, and all our efforts are wiped out.

An editor returns a manuscript for more details after I thought I'd done my best.

I catch a bad cold during a long-awaited vacation.

The clothes dryer goes on the fritz when overnight company is due any moment.

A young man at the door presses me to buy magazine subscriptions so he can fund tuition for college. I don't know him, and I don't want to buy anything, but then I feel guilty.

By the end of a week like this, I'm limping emotionally and spiritually. I know what you say, and I want to cling to it. But some days it's easier to do than others. Lord, give me your strength, please.

*[Jesus said,] "Now is your time of grief, but I will see you again and you will rejoice, and no one will take away your joy"* (John 16:22).

## Company's Coming

When I was younger, Lord, I loved having people over for dinner or for dessert and a table game. But now it seems like a lot of effort. Maybe we should keep it simple and all meet at a local restaurant and let someone else cook, serve, and then clean up after we leave. Of course that comes with a hefty price tag. It's definitely less expensive to eat at home, and at this time of year with holiday gifts to buy, we are watching our budget.

We also have such a beautiful set of dishes and serving bowls. Do I really want them to sit behind closed doors until I die and then go to my kids or to the Salvation Army? Why not pull them out and use them? Our friends love home-cooked meals because so many of them now eat out two or three times a week. And besides, I'm a good cook and my husband is a wonderful host. The table always shines when the guests arrive. Flowers, candles, sparkling water goblets, and polished silver are better than a welcome mat at the front door.

I'm feeling happy just thinking about how much fun it will be to entertain again. It's been a long time. What will I serve? Time to bring out my cookbooks and come up with a meal that is delicious, healthy, and easy to prepare. Economical too. Yep! I'm ready, dear Lord, and I pray you will bless the meal and our conversation around the table.

## All that Jazz

Lord, I like jazz. I have since I was in high school. Now I'm hooked on the piano renditions of Beegie Adair. I love her style and the songs she plays. She's over 70 and still recording and performing professionally. Some of my favorite CDs include *Save the Last Dance for Me, Moments to Remember, I'll Take Romance, Jazz for the Road,* and *Embraceable You.* Today I added to my collection with *Winter Romance.*

Music provides something that no other medium offers. I love snuggling with Charles on a cold winter's night with easy jazz playing in the background. While listening to a song, I can return to a former time as though it were yesterday. I recall the scent of April in Paris perfume, the feel of a crinoline underskirt to hold the flare of a street dress or prom gown, bouffant hairdos from the 1950s, white buck shoes and Bermuda shorts, as well as the warm embrace of a boyfriend while dancing at a party.

I'm an older woman now, God, but I have a young heart filled with romance and a desire for love, appreciation, and spontaneous fun. Thank you for giving me a spirit of playfulness and youth. May my passions always serve you!

> *You make known to me the path of life; you will fill me with joy in your presence, with eternal pleasures at your right hand* (Psalm 16:11).

## Prayer Walk

Lord, I love it when my husband and I go for a prayer walk. We tool around our community at a good clip, while at the same time praying for family, friends, neighbors, and the world at large. We can't cover all the needs, but you can! I know you use our words to partner with you in bringing about changes in the lives of others as well as our own.

Prayer has transformed my life for sure. For many years I didn't pray much, except by rote when at a church service or at a healing conference. But now, just as I'm doing right here in this book, I'm praying to you about what's on my heart. I'm having a heartfelt conversation with you as I bring my hopes, and dreams, and worries, and concerns to your open hand. Thank you that praying is as easy as letting my thoughts turn into words.

When I first heard that you told your followers to pray without ceasing, I have to admit it sounded like a tall order—one I'd never be able to fulfill. After all, I had a family to look after, a home to keep in order, and friendships to maintain. Maybe I could insert a prayer here and there while waiting in a carpool line or driving to the grocery store, but praying *without ceasing*? That means never stopping, keeping on, focusing on you day and night. It seemed impossible.

Now, however, I understand your command. You are asking me to remain in a state of prayer, in close touch with you, speaking to you as the words come, keeping my communication with you fluid and friendly so I can hear as well as speak. Thank you for opening my ears and eyes to prayer and to prayer walks.

## More to Come

Sometimes, Lord, it's fun to watch infomercials on TV. There is always something new to buy for the kitchen, bathroom, or garage. I rarely place an order, but I get a kick out of the gadgets that inventors come up with. In the 1970s, a late-night marketer named Barry Becher demonstrated and promoted the Ginsu knife. His spiel was so effective that by the mid-1980s his company had taken in more than $500 million in sales revenue. "But wait, there's more!" became a popular slogan associated with his sales pitch. The announcer shouted the four words before throwing in a few extras to anyone who purchased the miracle knife.

I'm thinking of that famous phrase today and how it fits your promises of *more to come* after our life on earth:

*Listen, I tell you a mystery: We will not all sleep, but we will all be changed—in a flash, in the twinkling of an eye, at the last trumpet. For the trumpet will sound, the dead will be raised imperishable, and we will be changed...then the saying that is written will come true: "Death has been swallowed up in victory"* (2 Corinthians 15:51-57).

It's one thing to be given an extra gadget free of charge. It's quite another to be given eternal life with you in heaven because of what you did on the cross for me.

## Hot Tea

For the Brits and the Irish, teatime is special. Coming from an Irish heritage, I'm a tea drinker. So thank you for this comforting beverage, dear Lord. There's nothing quite like a hot cup on a cold, winter afternoon. I like to sip tea between chapters of a book or after a row of knitting stitches. It warms my body and my spirit. Things settle down within me as the hot liquid permeates my being. I can think straight, work out a problem, consider an option, come to a decision, or make a new choice. Yes, tea it is—the drink of the day! Good for what ails me inside as the wind whips up on the outside.

## Pressure Cooker

I look at my daughters these days and see myself of years ago—rushing about, driving here and there, rustling up a meal before an evening meeting, tending to a cut, walking the dog, changing the linens, and on it goes. One chore follows another until it's time to fall into bed. Sometimes it's just too much. Life feels like a pressure cooker about to explode.

I asked a few friends how they keep the lid on. One says she knits at least two rows a day. Another takes a hot bath with the door locked to keep out kids and dogs. One woman said a long walk and a piece of chocolate do the trick for her. All those activities sound good to me—especially the chocolate! And most everyone admitted that at least a minute or two of prayer each day goes a long way to soothe the stress.

We're in a different kind of pressure cooker now that we're older. The kids are grown, and some of us have outlived our pets. We don't have to shop for groceries as often as we did when the house was full, and we can take an afternoon nap if we want to. But there's the pain in our backs, or weak knees, or a hearing problem, or thinning hair to contend with. The important remedy is still the same—time with you, O Lord. You take away the worry, the fear, the concern. You grant us peace. All we have to do is ask. I'm asking today.

## Small Talk

I dropped by my neighbor's house today. Hadn't seen her in weeks. How can this happen, Lord? We live on the same block, walk and drive the same streets, and shop at the same grocery store. So today we shared a few minutes of news. Small talk. Nothing important. Or was it? Connecting with people is important. Essential, actually. You were so good at this. You walked the byways chatting with the common folk as well as the leaders of your time, sharing a meal, a cup of water, a word of encouragement, never too busy to hear people's concerns and feelings and worries. And you are never too busy to hear mine. Thank you for the example you provide to stop, look at, and listen to others like you did on earth and still do through your Holy Spirit. Checking in with my friends may be the best gift I can give.

## Thorny Issue

Our beautiful climbing ice rose is bare. I miss the white blooms that lit up our yard all summer long, adding special fragrance and petals to our landscape. I look forward to its return. Right now, though, it's time to hibernate for winter, to be still, to store up energy for the next season. This plant has much to teach me about shedding the old, preparing for the new, and, in the meantime, just *being*. I'm a doer, not a person usually content just to be. Maybe this winter I can work on that. And when I forget, you will remind me to step outside and take a look at this kindred plant that reveals your Spirit. Thank you, God, for the gifts of wisdom I find in your bountiful creation.

## "Wearywart"

Lord, I've come to you many times as a worrywart, but today I come as a "wearywart." I'm just plain tired—even though I had a good night's sleep after the grandkids left. To them, going to bed at 10:30 is no big deal. But to me it's huge. I like to slip into bed by 9:00 or 9:30. I made an exception last night, as I sometimes do, but I sure feel it today.

Please refresh my body and spirit, dear God. Give me a second wind. Keep me moving through the day so I can accomplish what I've set out to do and then close up shop early enough to grab a couple of extra hours of sleep tonight. And may I shut my eyes with a prayer of thanks on my lips as you remind me from your Word to have a sweet sleep.

## Wanted: Grace

Lord, I've been one of your followers for 30 years, and still I slip and slide from time to time. I need your grace desperately. I get up in the morning eager to be all that you've made me to be, and yet before noon there I go entertaining an unwanted thought or tossing a careless word across the room to my husband. I'm so aware of how helpless I am without you at my side every moment of the day. Thank you for smiling through these times with me. Or is that a sigh I detect?

## Snowshoes and Leggings

Lord, for some reason a picture of me pulling on my leggings and winter boots has popped into my mind. I can still remember the navy-blue color of the bulky pants and how I hated wearing them. But Mother insisted, so I couldn't go out the door without them. I recall the time in kindergarten when she made me wear knee-high socks, which I folded down to my ankles the minute I was on the school bus and out of her sight.

I'm wondering if this behavior is a metaphor for how I am with you sometimes. You guide my actions with your Word, and I listen attentively for a little while. But then I do what I please when I think you're not looking. How embarrassing to think of myself as a naughty child—especially now that I'm over 70 years old. Thank you for not giving up on me. I want to listen, and obey, and do what needs to be done—even when I don't feel like it.

## Rest in Peace, Marilyn

Lord, thank you for taking Marilyn home to you. She suffered so much in this life. I'm happy knowing she is at peace. What a joy it was to spend time with her last November. I'm so glad you prompted me to add that visit to my trip to Southern California. I had no idea it might be the last time we'd see each other. Writing was important to her, and how wonderful that I could include some of her stories in my books. I know that brought her a lot of joy. And now I have them to remind me of her.

## Curbside Prayer

Lord, I'm thinking of the time a cab driver paused for a moment at the curb before dropping my husband and me off at the airport in Dallas. We'd had such a good conversation during the ride that by the time we had to part company, we felt like old friends and were truly sorry to say goodbye. But then we chuckled, acknowledging that we'd have another chance to connect—in heaven!—where there would be no rushing, no goodbyes, no departures.

That's what I love about bumping into brothers and sisters in Christ. We're friends right out the gate. We may not live near one another, share the same backgrounds, or even speak the same language, but we're bound together nonetheless. A chance meeting like the one we encountered provided food for my soul for all the years since. Thank you for the body of Christ.

## Fresh Start

Lord, I remember one day lying facedown on the floor of my home office and crying out to you that I just couldn't do my job anymore—at least not in the way I'd been doing it. I was envious of other accomplished writers who were selling books, traveling, and speaking all over the place...yada, yada...and here I was after three decades still struggling to get by.

After spilling all my hurt and pain and shame, I did something I should have done much sooner: I let go of my hold on my life and gave it all to you. I surrendered my entire professional life—my whole life, actually—and I asked you to be my heavenly agent.

I sat up and felt lighter and freer than ever before! Suddenly it was time to live a life of gratitude, not just write and talk about it. Best of all, I had you, dear Jesus, as my friend, and I knew I was a friend of yours. With you being for me, who can be against me? From that day to this—some five years later—I've never wanted for anything. Your abundance surrounds me physically, financially, and spiritually. Thank you, God, for showing me the way to lasting peace and confidence.

## Something to Smile About

Lord, remember how I seldom smiled when I was a child? I was shy, embarrassed to be seen, lacking in confidence. I didn't know I was your beloved daughter. Mom prodded me, telling me I had a beautiful smile and pretty dimples. But it didn't change things. I held back—until that day years later when I learned that you loved me so much you died on the cross for me so that I could be with you for all eternity. That's something to smile about and share with others!

Now I smile all the time. It's a gift. It might not *look* like one since it doesn't come wrapped in pretty paper, but it's a gift nonetheless. When people smile at me, I light up inside. I feel better about myself and about my day. Now I know that can happen for them too when I share my smile.

So let me go about my life, dear God, with a smile in my heart and on my lips so that everyone I encounter will feel a little closer to you.

## A Good Book

I love to sit up in bed at night with a great book or lounge by the fire after a day's work and read. One of the best parts, Lord, is connecting with you at such times. When I read a prairie romance by Jeanette Oke, or a cozy mystery by Lorena McCourtney, or an inspiring and deep story of life in today's world by Karen Kingsbury, I find you on every page. I see your love and forgiveness displayed in the lives of fictional characters as they fall, or sin, or make poor choices, and then repent and lead changed lives. I think of your mercies that are new every morning (Lamentations 3:23 NCV).

I'm grateful to those authors who make it possible for me to connect with you in ways that inspire and encourage me to live an honorable life that will be a blessing to everyone I encounter. Thank you for good books and talented storytellers.

## Holiday Shopping

I hustled through the mall, breezing in and out of various stores, eager to locate the perfect gifts for family and friends. Lord, I felt you with me on this mission that seemed impossible at the time. But as I relaxed into the task instead of letting anxiety take over, I saw your love in the faces of people I met, your creativity displayed in the decorations and music, and your Spirit reflected in the joy of children and parents spending time together.

These loving examples of your presence helped me calm down and slow my pace as I realized that you'd lead me to just the right places. *"The LORD makes firm the steps of the one who delights in him"* (Psalm 37:23). So there was no need to be consumed with checking things off my to-do list. It would all work out if I kept my focus on you and listened for your gentle leading—even when shopping for gifts.

I'm so glad I took the time to enjoy the visual feast and the happy sounds all around me, as well as stopping for a short break at a little café to sip a latte while I made a list and checked it twice before carrying on. Thank you, God, for being with me—even in a busy mall during the holidays.

## A Sleepless Night

Lord, here I am wide awake at two o'clock in the morning because I'm troubled by a decision I have to make. I hate this. I need my sleep. Yet the more I try to relax, the worse I feel. Things seem so much larger and worrisome in the dark. Why don't I turn to you for guidance? you remind me. Of course! That's the solution that tossing and turning can never deliver.

This is the perfect time to ask for guidance and wisdom. My husband snores softly beside me, and the neighbors are all quiet and tucked in. The only sound is the distant wailing of a cat. In the still of the night, your words come to me from the Bible: *"I will lead them in paths they have not known: I will make darkness light before them and crooked things straight"* (Isaiah 42:16).

It's all about trust, isn't it, God? I've read that verse many times before, but it's more real to me in this moment. With your words to comfort me, I will go to sleep in the dark, confident that my answer will be here in the light of morning.

## Favorite Foods

My eight-year-old grandson asked me to make his favorite dish—Easy Chicken and Mini Penne Casserole. Of course I agreed! I invited him and his family over to our house so we could enjoy the meal together. That afternoon as I prepared the chicken and pasta, the sauce and the vegetable, and the apple crisp for later, I realized you were in the kitchen with me. I felt happy, and grateful, and excited to entertain the family with nourishing food. And I loved being asked to do something that would please my grandson—just as I know, God, that it's your pleasure to do things that please your children.

The next morning I asked my husband what he'd like for breakfast. "Oatmeal with nuts and fruit, yogurt and maple syrup," he said, "like you usually make. It's my favorite."

A few minutes later I was in the kitchen and, once again while cooking, there you were, dear Lord. What a nice feeling to serve my husband what he wants and what's healthy too. How easy it has become to give to others freely without expecting anything in return.

## Ah! Art

As I walked through one art gallery after another, I found your presence in the art I admired, my God. The lifelike paintings by the old masters as well as those of contemporary artists inspired me. Many beautiful pieces reflected stories from the Bible, including

"The Story of Ruth" by Thomas Matthews Rooke (1876) and "Sarah presenting Hagar to Abraham" by Adriaen van der Werff (1699).

Just as you motivated the work of their hands, I felt motivated to reflect on the great teachings each painting represented. During the artists' day, people learned about you, the lessons you imparted, and how to pray as a result of viewing these blessed works on canvas, and in sculpture, as well as in the architecture of magnificent cathedrals. And many of those works are still here today for us to enjoy and appreciate. The more I view them, the greater the spiritual benefit.

> *[The* Lord*] has filled them with skill to do all kinds of work as engravers, designers, embroiderers in blue, purple and scarlet yarn and fine linen, and weavers—all of them skilled workers and designers* (Exodus 35:35).

## My Warm Sweater

I've had this old, black, "granny" sweater for 20 years at least. I still love it. The thick, cable-knit wool keeps me warm on cold, winter days...and even on mild ones when I'm indoors and sitting still at the computer. Thank you, God, for the sheep that provided this garment of warmth, for the machines that stitched the yarn together, and the hands that packaged it. Some things I don't ever want to get rid of, and this is one of them. Maybe one of my grands will want it one day to remind him or her of me. I have other treasures to pass on, but this is unique because it's such a part of *me*. I've lived in it for years. It has seen me through tough times, and good times, and everything in-between. Some items are just too special to let go of. My old granny sweater is one of them.

# Mac and Cheese

My grandson visited me this week. His favorite lunch at my house is macaroni and cheese. There you were, dear God, with me as I fixed his meal (from a package, I admit). I thought about how you supply food for me and all your people in ways we aren't even aware of sometimes.

I remember when my husband and I were so lean on finances that I wondered if we'd have to stand in line at the food pantry at church—something I'd never done before. And I also worried that I'd be wearing the same clothes for the next two years. Silly me—to fret about whether or not you would come through for us, Lord.

One morning a young friend who had recently lost her mother to cancer came to my door carrying a huge box. "It would mean a lot to me," she said, "if you'd consider wearing some of my mother's clothes. I can't let go of them yet, and they appear to be about your size."

"It would be an honor." I took the package with gratitude. Everything she brought fit me perfectly! I wore those outfits for the next year, at least.

At Christmas that year my husband and I were without work. My freelance writing jobs had slowed to a drizzle, and my husband had lost his employment when the company he worked for closed its doors. Once more you showed up, dear God. Friends from our prayer group contributed $300 to our holiday fare and an anonymous donor made arrangements for us to receive $500 in cash toward our rent. No one can out-give you, Lord, when it comes to food, clothing, rent money, or whatever else is needed—including mac and cheese for my grandson.

## Sea Creatures

One of the most enjoyable things for us to do on a day off is visit the Monterey Bay Aquarium. As I move from one exhibit to another, it's easy to see your imprint, dear Lord, on these unique and beautiful creatures of the sea, especially my favorite—the sea otter. Abby was a new addition to the otter family, after having been stranded on Jalama Beach in Northern Santa Barbara County five years ago. Now she's a responsible adult being trained to be a surrogate mother and companion to other rescued pups before they are returned to the wild.

I enjoy watching Abby play with kelp and eat frozen treats. But as I observe her antics and those of her furry friends and then read about the role she plays with displaced otters, I'm reminded of how you provide for displaced persons too: *"The Lord protects and preserves the strangers and temporary residents, He upholds the fatherless and the widow and sets them upright, but the way of the wicked He makes crooked (turns upside down and brings to ruin)"* (Psalm 146:9 AMP).

Sometimes I feel displaced—especially now that I'm an older woman. Young people have taken over the world. My adult children don't need me as much as they once did, and I don't see them as often as I'd like. I'm not as agile as I was, and I tire more easily than just a few years ago. But then I remember that, like Abby, I'm a responsible adult—an older, responsible adult. It's my time now to be a companion and caring friend to the pups in my life, such as younger women who need guidance and a positive role model.

If you provide protection and care for the animals of your kingdom, how much more you will look out for your people! From the odd-looking ocean sunfish to the great white shark, from the orphan to the widow, from the young to the old, you are here, dear God.

## Missionary Hearts

Lord, thank you for the special week we had with the visiting missionaries from Taiwan. We opened our guest room to them, not knowing what to expect until they walked through our front door. What a wonderful surprise! They were a delightful couple, filled with stories of their work among the Taiwanese and eager to hear about our lives here in the States. It's such a blessing to interact with people who are out in the field sharing the gospel with men and women who might never hear about you otherwise.

Their visit prompted me to be more aware of the mission field right here in my community. Help me use the opportunities you present to share my experiences of your love and care and your promise of eternal life for all who come to you and follow you as Lord. I particularly want to reach out to older people so they will find out about you before their lives are over.

## Mentor and Mentee

Lord, today I'm thinking about the mentors in my life—from my kindergarten teacher to my counselor in college and beyond, women and men who have spoken into my life in a way that has helped me grow, thrive, and then give back to others what was given to me. I remember the woman I spoke with regularly on the phone when I was new in my faith. Day after day she listened to my worries and problems and then pointed me to a verse in the Bible that would help me aspire to a higher level of living. She encouraged me to lean on you instead of on me. Sometimes just her example was enough. She preached without saying a word!

*Teach the older women to be reverent in the way they live,*
*not to be slanderers or addicted to much wine, but to teach*

*what is good. Then they can urge the younger women to love their husbands and children, to be self-controlled and pure* (Titus 2:3-5).

Years later I met a young woman who, like myself at her age, was struggling with divorce, finances, raising kids, and marrying again. I knew it was my turn to give back some of the good wisdom that my mentor had instilled in me. Today this young woman and I meet once a month. We talk about life, about your promises, and about some of the steps we can take to live better lives for you. It feels good to share with her my experiences, hope, and faith in you—and then watch her make progress on her own path. Thank you for the gift of mentors and mentees.

## Divorce

Lord, I was so angry when another woman came into my first husband's life. She'd made a play for him, and he was happy to follow, leaving the kids and me in the dust. Little did I imagine there would come a time when I could say to another hurting person, "You *can* find God during your divorce." But now I can because that's what happened to me. You graciously came into my life at that dreadful time that occurred during a Christmas season years ago—a time I wanted to spend making happy memories with my children.

At first I couldn't envision life beyond what I'd known for 20 years. But you had me covered, not only when the marriage ended but well after that. *"For I know the plans I have for you,' declares the Lord, 'plans to prosper you and not to harm you, plans to give you hope and a future'"* (Jeremiah 29:11). When I read that verse, I made it mine, clinging to it day after day, realizing that nothing could happen to me that you didn't first know about, and that, as your child, I had nothing to fear. You would always provide for me.

Lord, today I ask that you give strength and courage to those who are going through divorces. Wrap these people in your arms and hold them close as you did for me. Be especially present to my friend who is divorcing after nearly 50 years of marriage. She is no longer a young woman. She will need you to stand with her as she faces a totally new way of life. Thank you that you love my friend and that you'll be her rock and salvation.

## That Sinking Feeling

Lord, some of the things that are happening lately are pretty funny but also pretty scary. Are they going to get worse as I grow older? I'm afraid so! Remember the time I reached for an antibiotic cream instead of shaving cream to shave my legs? Or the time I poured myself a cup of syrup instead of coffee? It did seem a bit thick! Or what about the day I reached for my camera and wondered why the old-fashioned telephone in my hand wouldn't snap a photo. (Today, of course, I can take a picture with a smart phone.)

Tell me I'm not hopeless, Lord. And if you can't tell me that, please fill me with your hope so I'll know I'm going to make it through this aging thing.

> *Even to your old age and gray hairs I am he, I am he who will sustain you* (Isaiah 46:4).

## Bad News

O God, what else? I almost hate to open the newspaper. Today I was drawn into the tragedy of the dozens of people killed at a soccer match in Egypt, the fighting in Syria, the mud-slinging among American presidential candidates, and the four Britons who admitted conspiring to plant a bomb at the London Stock Exchange.

And yet the more I read, the more I see your presence in the midst of the bad news. You bring *good news*. As the Creator of the universe and the Author of Life, you rescue us from sin, heal our hurts, cover us with love, and restore us to sanity. You're not a dictator, so yes, bad things will happen to good people and bad, but you are always available to help us through our distress.

Knowing that, I'm trying to read about and listen to world events in a new way. Instead of being upset and depressed, I'm making it a habit to turn to you for guidance and grace and wisdom. At times like this, I take comfort in the "Serenity Prayer" by American theologian Reinhold Niebuhr that is popular in 12-Step Recovery Programs:

> God grant us the serenity to accept the things we cannot change, the courage to change the things we can, and the wisdom to know the difference.

## The Bounce-Back Factor

Lord, I like what Dr. Edward Creagan of the Mayo Clinic said in a recent issue of *Embody Health*, the clinic's newsletter. "Resiliency" is what he most admires about cancer patients who are able to focus on what is really important despite their illness. "Also known as the bounce-back factor, *resiliency* is the ability to take a big hit psychologically, spiritually, physically or financially and somehow move forward," he reported. It seems these men and women have been able to find you, God, during their illness.

It's never easy to face a health crisis or to endure tests and treatment that are often painful and unpleasant for days at a time. But to find you right there with them brings peace, courage, and a willingness to take each new day as it comes. Your Word says, *"I will never leave you nor forsake you"* (Hebrews 13:5). I pray for my friends and family members who are ill. Guide and comfort them, dear Lord, and give them your peace that passes all understanding.

## Popcorn and a Movie

It's that time of year, Lord. Time to make a batch of popcorn, put in a DVD, sink into the sofa, and hold hands with my hubby while watching a movie. When we were younger, we were all about driving to a local theater, standing in line for tickets, watching the movie, maybe going out to eat afterward, and then falling into bed late at night. But not anymore. Now, dear Lord, we're happiest when we're home at night with a little fire in the fireplace and the company of each other. We feel your presence at such times in a different way than usual. You seem to be telling us to relax and to rest in you as we let go of the day's tasks and ease off our stress load before going to bed. I like to think about Proverbs 3:24 at such times: *"When you lie down, you will not be afraid; when you lie down, your sleep will be sweet."*

## Hero No More

Things have changed between my youngest grandson and me. I used to be his hero. He loved it when I took him to the park, slid down the slide holding him around his belly, and stopped at a local ice cream shop for a treat. We'd sit at a small table, lick our ice cream cones, and talk about whatever crossed our minds. Lord, he'd even sing to me as I drove, and tears sometimes slid down my face as I thought about how quickly he'd be growing up. His world would widen, and it would include more and more people. *Would there still be room for me?* I wondered. Maybe not, so I'd better make the most of these days and months and years we have together.

Well, dear God, that growing-up time came sooner than I expected. The boy is now tech savvy! He's loaded my iPhone with a bunch of free game apps—with my permission, of course. So now when I drive him home from school or to the beach, we hardly talk anymore. He's playing with his super heroes on the screen, and I'm feeling like chopped liver. Oh well, I had his undivided attention when I had it. I take comfort in remembering that I used to be his hero.

## Shout-Outs from Heaven

Lord, thank you for checking in each day and providing your wisdom and guidance. I think of your messages as shout-outs from heaven. When I'm in a tough spot, I give a shout and you shout back just what I need to hear. I like your reminder today that you're God and I'm not. How could I forget? If I settle down and listen, I always hear what I need. And if I follow your suggestions, I'm set for the day. So today I will keep in mind (with your help) that you're in charge of the universe (including me), and that as long as I follow you, I'll be all right. So far so good! I love you, Lord.

## New Life

Lord, every few weeks we receive a card in the mail from a local charity soliciting used clothing, furniture, and household items to help those in need. These are good reminders to share what I have, to let go of items I'm no longer using, and to give of what I love. It's easy to hand over things I'm finished with, but how much nicer to give from my pile of treasures. So this season I will look through my books, and sweaters, and shoes, and jackets and give some away so another person can be warm, cozy, and refreshed.

## Out with the Old

Lord, nature is hibernating, storing up treasure and energy for new growth in the spring. Maybe I should follow this example. It's time to rid myself of old behaviors, stale ways of thinking, and outdated habits. It's also time for a good housecleaning—the kind where I go behind the sofa, get under the bed, and move around the corners chasing out the dust bunnies that clutter my home. On second thought, maybe I'll hire someone to do all that. I'll use the time to take a walk and talk with you!

## In with the New

Lord, what a perfect opportunity I will have next week to begin anew. I'm going to a retreat in Monterey with other authors and friends. I promise to make the most of lovely walks, sitting on a bench overlooking the ocean, sleeping peacefully, and praying quietly, knowing you're with me in everything I think, say, and do. May I return home a new woman in you!

## Say What You Mean

Yesterday I was reminded of how important it is to say what I mean—without being mean. I was in a tiff with my son, Lord, and I really didn't like it. I love my kids and never want to upset them. But something I said or the way I said it set him off. It took a few back-and-forth emails for us to reconcile. For a moment there I was afraid he'd unfriend me on Facebook! But he didn't go that far. He asked me to be *honest*, but when I was, it didn't go over very well.

I can't help but think about how that happens with you and me too. You always say what you mean, and you're never mean about it. But I take it that way sometimes, especially when I want an answer to a prayer right here and now and you don't respond immediately. Or when I feel nudged to rest in you, to settle down and wait. It was all I could do to keep my fingers from flying across the keyboard this week when I was annoyed with an editor I'm working with. I wanted to provoke a response, but you encouraged me to wait. I did, but I didn't like it. And then the very next day I heard from him. Not only did he have an answer to my question, he presented me with another writing opportunity. How foolish it would have been for me to act on my emotions when the right thing to do was act from my mind. Thank you for always saying what you mean— without being mean.

## Alone but Not Lonely

Lord, thank you for showing me I can be alone yet not feel lonely. It happened last weekend when my husband was out of town. I had a couple of projects I wanted to tackle, as well as cleaning our house. It was quiet around here with just you and me, and I loved it. I enjoyed being able to eat, sleep, pray, watch television, and write without anyone to think about but myself. It was a nice change. I'm not ready for this to be permanent though. Please don't take my husband to heaven yet. But a respite now and then is delightful. I'm no longer afraid of being alone because it's not the same as being lonely.

## Strength for Today

Lord, my prayer is for strength today. I'll ask again tomorrow for the amount I need then. And the next and the next. I won't pray for a lifetime supply because then I might go off on my own and forget to return to you. I do best when I'm in touch with you on a daily basis, knowing that you are my source and my supply, and that you give as needed when needed. How blessed I am to know you as my Lord and Savior.

## Walk Humbly

My goal, dear God, is to walk humbly with you. But you know me better than I know myself. You know I get stuck sometimes, giving in to fear, worrying about what others think, and then performing instead of being real. I forget to stick close to you. What you think of me is all that matters. Knowing you are beside me makes all things right. Help me show your love to others instead of trying to get them to love me. Remind me often to obey your commandments and leave the rest to you. That sounds good to me! May I carry that out according to your will.

## Silk Milk?

I've heard of silk sheets and silk scarves, but now there's "silk milk." It's made from soy. Why not call it by its proper name—soy milk? That's the trouble with this society. We don't say it like it is. We have to dress up or dress down items, from food to furniture, in order to create intrigue or a hook to convince people to buy. What's next, Lord? I don't remember my parents being faced with so many choices. They went to the grocery store and bought milk, bread, eggs, meat, fruits, and vegetables, and that was that. But today the choices are so vast and varied! I need a clear head and a clear list to make it from one aisle to the next and stay on budget.

I thank you for even being in the supermarket to help me be discerning with my purchases. My fridge and pantry may not be as full as some others, but what we need we have. And it's been good for our waistlines too. We eat less and weigh less, but we're content. Thank you for the gift of discernment.

## A New Son

Thank you again, God, for bringing Tigotac into our lives. We may never meet in person, but he is alive in our hearts. I like hearing about his schooling and his family. But most of all, I like that he's learning about you and your love for him. Being a sponsor is a special role—not only for this new son, but for Charles and me as well. We get to contribute money and prayer to this young life. May you direct and guide him and us, dear Lord, as we continue our relationship through Compassion, a ministry dedicated to releasing children from poverty. What a privilege!

## Money Mania

Lord, why do I keep noodling you about our income? You said you'd provide, so that should be that…'nuf said. But I don't live by it. I just talk about it. I lay down the burden for a while and then pick it up again. You must grow weary of my worrying. I sure do. The Bible says, *"Keep your lives free from the love of money and be content with what you have, because God has said, 'Never will I leave you; never will I forsake you'"* (Hebrews 13:5). I need to read this more often and write it across my heart.

## Another Deadline

You always prove yourself faithful, O God. Just when I wondered what earning opportunity you'd send my way, it arrived in the form of two short book assignments. I didn't pray for these specific tasks, but they came to me nevertheless—thanks to you. I look forward to what I will learn and how I will grow as a writer because of these projects. Guide my fingers over the keyboard, Lord, and open my mind to the words I should put on each page. I pray for the young students who will read these books, that they will be blessed by the text and photos and come closer to you as they learn about the animals you created.

## Barbecued Chicken

I'm making barbecued chicken for dinner tonight—one of our favorite dishes. I'd better keep my head on straight, dear God, when I pull out the sauce from the fridge or I might make the same mistake a friend of mine made. She doused her chicken legs with chocolate syrup. You might say the result was finger-lickin' good, but it wasn't what her guests expected. And I'd better pay attention when I'm baking potatoes to go with the chicken thighs or the spuds could end up in the freezer instead of the oven. You can't trust me these days…I'm a senior, you know.

## Cheery Platitudes

On a day like today the last thing a hurting friend needs is a cheery platitude such as "God's in charge" or "Buck up. This too will pass." Often the best thing to do is stand or sit with a friend who is in pain and just listen. But ouch! That's hard to do sometimes. I have so many good ideas and wise words for other people. I ought to turn around and share them with myself and then see if I heed my own advice before dispensing it to those around me. Thanks, Lord, for keeping a close watch on me so I don't get carried away with my own version of wisdom.

## Vent Cleaning

The doorbell rang, and I knew it was time for the dreaded appointment. The repairman had arrived to clean the clothes dryer vent. That meant pulling out the machine, blowing out the accumulated lint, cleaning up the mess that such a task involves, and, worst of all, shelling out more than $200 for the job. All that on top of a washing machine repair that will cost more than $400, a cleaning crew for nearly $500, new batteries for the smoke alarms, property taxes, and auto and home insurance payments now due. And we need someone to come and inspect and clean our built-in fireplace. Yikes! Thousands of dollars out the door in a matter of days. All this just before holiday shopping and entertaining and all the outlay that includes.

Okay, Lord, I'm finished venting. Now I can laugh! I make a big deal out of such trivia—trivia in terms of the big picture. You've got us covered. The money is there for each need, and more will come. I'm sure of it because you always provide—even if sometimes in the nick of time. Thank you for that! And thank you that I can verbalize my concerns without you becoming upset with me. You are good all the time.

## Winter Walk

I took a walk today, but it was so windy and cold I came back home within 15 minutes. What a little chicken I am! People in some parts of the world would think our weather was warm compared to theirs. But it was such a contrast to last week when we had five days of surprising temps—from the mid-seventies to 90 degrees! I loved it. But I confess, Lord, that on one of the days I came back within 15 minutes as well. Why? It was too hot!

Aren't I hard to please? You must be throwing up your hands right now wondering what I want. I'll tell you. How about mid-seventies? That would be perfect. But, of course, it is up to you to calm the sea, stir the breeze, coax the sun, and bring the wind and rain. It is for me to receive what you order and be grateful. So thank you for knowing what is needed and when, and then supplying it at the perfect time.

## A Mouthful

Lord, how funny it was to see my granddaughter with chipmunk cheeks after her dental surgery last week. She had four wisdom teeth pulled in one day. No wonder her face swelled up and she felt crummy. I teased her about losing her wisdom. In her state of pain, however, she didn't think it was funny. Sometimes, though, a smile, chuckle, or good belly laugh can be just what is needed when we're suffering.

I like the Martin Luther quote I read last week: "If they don't allow laughter in heaven, then I don't want to go there." I'm with Marty. I want to know there will be reasons to laugh and play in heaven, that heaviness will be forever gone, and that all God's children will be friends. Perhaps this Bible verse from Luke's gospel applies: *"Blessed are you who weep now, for you will laugh"* (6:21). That says something to me about what heaven will be like. I'm already looking forward to that joyful reunion.

## Words Worth Hearing

Dear God, thank you for giving me the words of your mouth—the ones worth hearing—when I spoke last week at the Fall Brunch at church. It was such a neat experience to stand before the audience and know that what I shared you already approved of and enjoyed. I loved smiling and laughing with the men and women and seeing how a touch of humor can go a long way toward bringing people together.

Afterward, men and women streamed to my book table, eager to tell me their funny experiences. Older folks like to talk about their lives and compare them to those of newer generations. In our minds, our growing-up years were better than those of anyone alive today. To many, the younger crowd is going to the dogs. But I'm wondering if our parents didn't think the same thing about us when we were young.

The most important thing for me to remember is that *you*, Lord, are the same yesterday, today, and forever. With that in mind, how could I worry even for a minute what will happen in the future?

## Grace Alone

Yesterday, dear Lord, I watched a character in a movie give his life to drugs and alcohol. He nearly died before he woke up to the fact that he'd lived a lie most of his 50-something years. You know I don't drink and I've never used drugs, but I sure have given hunks of my life over to one addiction or another during my life—eating, trying to control outcomes, giving advice, people-pleasing, and more. Thankfully, I'm in recovery now and leaning on you instead of on people and things. I pray today for everyone in the throes of alcoholism, or overeating, or drugs, or gambling, or whatever has them in the grip of dependency. May you reach each one, God, with your loving touch and your grace and forgiveness. Give them the strength to be overcomers.

## Restoration

My friend wrote to me, Lord, to share her good news. She's feeling great after her surgery. Thank you for restoring her body and renewing her life. Her courage and perseverance have inspired me. I don't know that I would be as brave as she's been while going through chemo and radiation and feeling sick so often during the process. But you were there with her, and she felt your presence. No one can do what you can do, dear God. I am grateful for your healing touch.

## Cold Nights

I'm visiting my sister this week, and though the days are still hot here in Southern California, the nights are cold. I awakened in the middle of the night and pulled up an extra blanket. It felt good to snuggle deep into the comforting warmth. This reminded me, dear God, of your blanket of love, there for the taking whenever I feel scared, lonely, or uncertain. I can lean into you and feel your presence no matter where I am. Thank you for that ever-available assurance.

You promised you'd send the Comforter after you returned to heaven to sit at the right hand of your Father, and you kept that promise. I'm confident that whenever I call on your name, you are here with me—Father, Son, and Holy Spirit—to guide, guard, and govern me.

It feels good to tuck myself into a fluffy down comforter when I go to bed at night, but nothing can comfort my spirit like your Holy Spirit—the true Comforter.

## Hot Food

My sister and I had fun today preparing lunch together. I took over the salad, and she stir-fried the veggies and warmed the leftover chicken. The meal was delicious! But it can't compare to the food you provide, dear God, for my body and my soul. Your promises and your presence feed my spirit with wisdom, confidence, and encouragement. Within a few hours my stomach will rumble and my body will need another round of nourishment, but when you feed me I'm content forever, never running out, never feeling deprived again. Still, I long for more of you, and my passion is to immerse myself in your Word. Thank you for taking care of my physical needs, God, but more important, thank you for feeding my spirit. May I always be in tune with you.

# Winter Worship

Lord, I'm looking at a card I received in the church bulletin this week announcing a Celtic Christmas Concert that will take place in a couple of weeks. I look forward to this time of celebration and worship as we officially enter the Christmas season. Churches all over the world will be hosting their own services this winter, ushering in the anniversary of the birth of Christ. I pray today that it will be a time of joy-filled praise, thoughtful prayer, and loving fellowship among all people. May the love you brought to earth through Jesus overcome bias and prejudice and opposition. Unite us in joyful songs of gratitude to you. Without you, dear God, we are nothing. With you, we are all we can be and have all we need and want. Praise you, Lord, from whom all blessings flow.

# A Good Talking To

I remember my mother sometimes saying that I needed what she called "a good talking to." I knew what that meant. I was going to be scolded…or reminded…or informed of something I'd neglected to do or needed to learn so she and I would be, as we say today, "on the same page." Lord, there are times when I imagine you'd like to say the same thing to me. I can use a scolding every now and then when I let a wayward thought get the best of me, or when I need to be reminded that you're God and I'm not, or when you want to inform me of a truth that I skipped over in my desire to do things my way. Thank you that I can always trust you to speak to me with love and grace and forgiveness so our talks lift me up to where you want me to be.

## Healing Prayer

Thank you, dear God, for the healing prayers for my sister last week. She didn't know what to expect from the service, and I wasn't sure either since the people directing the session and the location were both new to me. I did know all the worship songs, however, so that was special. I was able to get right into the spirit of things. The prayers my sister received increased her hope, and she seemed more upbeat when we left the church.

God, I pray that you will bring the healing you have for her, and that she will accept it with a grateful heart. It's difficult sometimes to let in the words and embrace their power. We've all been disappointed at times, and we tend to back away when people promise the moon. On the other hand, if we don't open our hearts and hands to you, how can we receive from you the very thing we want? It's crazy, isn't it? You, the Great Physician, have so much for us and yet we stand afraid.

I pray now, in Jesus' name, that you will soften our hearts and enlighten our minds so we not only hear about your miracles of healing but become one of those in whom a miracle of healing occurs when we need it. Thank you, God, for loving us so much.

## God Calling

Today my sister and I stopped at the phone store to look at the "next best thing." Chockfull of gadgets and gizmos, the latest smart phone is definitely it. I wanted my sister to buy one so we can play games together across cyberspace and keep in touch through text messaging, Facebook, and Twitter. She didn't go for it just yet. Maybe she needs more time.

And maybe I need some time to consider how dependent I've

become on my phone. I like to have it with me wherever I go. It holds my calendar, Bible, dictionary, music, notes, reminders, games, and more. I thank you for this advanced technology, but most of all I thank you for the direct line I have to you that relies on the Holy Spirit, not on Sprint or AT&T or Verizon.

## Prayer for a Friend

Lord, thank you for a wonderful visit with my friend. I'm so glad I could help her with household chores and cooking. We also had fun together walking, talking, and laughing. Laughter is such good medicine, especially in the winter of our lives when our inner landscape as well as the outer one can seem cold and barren.

Please, God, comfort and strengthen her. Give her your peace and the assurance of your presence in her life regardless of what comes her way. And for her husband I pray too that soon you will open the gates of heaven and welcome him home. He lingers in confusion and upset, wondering where he is and what he's supposed to do next. Only you know the answer to that. May he receive your guidance and comfort today.

## Better Than a Pill

I liked hearing what the doctor said about exercise—especially during the cold, rainy months when we don't feel like leaving the warmth and comfort of our homes. "Exercise is better than a pill," he proclaimed with confidence. "Get out there and walk, walk, walk." Amen to that! So I'm doing it—walking and praying and thanking you for the legs that carry me and the lungs that inhale and exhale the breath I need. What a privilege to be an older person who is still fit and happy! We never know what's coming, so I want to be diligent in my desire to keep doing what I can while I can, knowing that you are in charge and will always see that I'm cared for in whatever way is necessary.

## Big Bird

Lord, how funny that we focus so much of our attention on the birds that will grace most of our tables on Thanksgiving and/or Christmas. Recipes for brining, and baking, and stuffing, and serving are in store flyers, on websites, in blogs. But where do we advertise the most important part of all—giving thanks to you, our Master and Creator? Today I want to do that. I want to thank you in everything I think, say, and do. You are the author of all that I am and have. How blessed I've been throughout my life to feel your love and care and guidance. I love you, dear God, during this happy holiday season and all through the year.

## Kindness

Lord, as I think about the birth of your Son, Jesus, during this Christmas season I pray for a resurgence of kindness in our world, not only at this time of year but for every day. May people take up civility once again—using polite communication and simple courtesy toward one another. We all have so many needs and desires, but we often express them in such uncivil and selfish ways. We try to be funny at the expense of another person or make a comment that is insensitive or even downright offensive and then palm it off as a joke.

Let this change begin with me, God. Help me pay closer attention to the words I think and speak. If I can't say something positive and uplifting, poke me in the ribs so I'll know to be quiet. I know I'll fail from time to time, as all humans do, but if you refresh my memory and give me an extra helping of grace, I know things can change for the better. I pray so. Thank you for what you are doing and will do in my heart and the hearts of all people.

## Memories

Lord, on this cold, almost-winter night, I'm thinking of something my dad often said as we sat by the fire warming our toes and sipping hot chocolate. "All we have in the end are our memories, so make sure they're good ones." Now that I'm older, I see his point more clearly. He wanted us to live our lives in such a way that we would leave a heritage of good thoughts and delightful memories. I haven't been totally successful in this, but I'm working at it. Philippians 4:8 is good to ponder: *"Finally, brothers and sisters, whatever is true, whatever is noble, whatever is right, whatever is pure, whatever is lovely, whatever is admirable—if anything is excellent or praiseworthy—think about such things."* Help me, dear God, to do this each and every day so that I leave for my family and friends a treasury of special memories of our times together…with you at the center of each one.

# A Note from the Editors

We hope you enjoyed *Lord How Did I Get This Old So Soon?* by Karen O'Connor, published by the Books and Inspirational Media Division of Guideposts, a nonprofit organization that touches millions of lives every day through products and services that inspire, encourage, help you grow in your faith, and celebrate God's love.

Thank you for making a difference with your purchase of this book, which helps fund our many outreach programs to military personnel, prisons, hospitals, nursing homes, and educational institutions.

We also create many useful and uplifting online resources. Visit Guideposts.org to read true stories of hope and inspiration, access OurPrayer network, sign up for free newsletters, download free e-books, join our Facebook community, and follow our stimulating blogs.

To learn about other Guideposts publications, including the bestselling devotional *Daily Guideposts*, go to Guideposts.org/Shop, call (800) 932-2145, or write to Guideposts, PO Box 5815, Harlan, Iowa 51593.